Return to the Glen

Return to the Glen

Adventures on the Scotch Whisky Trail

By Richard Grindal
Photography by Catherine Karnow

Alvin Rosenbaum Projects, Inc.
Chevy Chase, Maryland

Return to the Glen,
Adventures on the Scotch Whisky Trail

Copyright ©1989: Text by Richard Grindal Photography by Catherine Karnow

Editors: Nancy L. Johnson and Leonard Sherp
Designer: Kathleen Mary Hardesty

ISBN 0-9623639-0-1

Published in the United States by
Alvin Rosenbaum Projects, Inc.
Chevy Chase, Maryland

Printed in Hong Kong by
South Sea International Press Ltd.

Photographs:
Page 2: In the glen of the Livet
Page 5: The Machrie Golf Course, Islay
Page 6: Along the Whisky Trail
Page 7: John The Hod, a deerstalker, the West Highlands
Pages 8-9: Fishermen, the Highlands
Page 10: Barley field near Rothes
Page 11: Fisherman on Skye

Alvin Rosenbaum Projects, Inc. would like to thank the following
for their support during the preparation of this book:

HERTZ EUROPE LTD.
BRITISH AIRWAYS
SKEABOST HOUSE HOTEL, ISLE OF SKYE, SCOTLAND
THE ROTHES GLEN HOTEL, ROTHES, SCOTLAND
THE TULCHAN LODGE, GRANTOWN-ON-SPREY, SCOTLAND
GROSVENOR HOUSE, LONDON, ENGLAND
THE MINMORE LODGE, GLENLIVET, SCOTLAND

Contents

The Anatomy of Scotch

A doctor friend of mine, Hamish, tells me of how once while lecturing to medical students in Edinburgh—the theme of this lecture is not entirely clear to me and may not have been to him either—he digressed and began speaking of the virtues of drinking alcohol. Scotch whisky, he told his audience, is good for the health and amongst other things is an excellent tranquillizer. Why are doctors, he wondered, not allowed to prescribe a good dram every night for their patients? It would be much better for the patients than all the sedatives and sleeping pills which are now being dispensed to those who find difficulty in sleeping and a good deal less expensive for the Health Service.

In question-time after his talk, he was immediately confronted by a student who was clearly a convinced teetotaller—yes, we have them in Scotland too. Surely, the student demanded, the lecturer was not suggesting that whisky could be beneficial to health? Hamish replied mildly that yes, research showed that a modest amount of alcohol every day helped to protect against coronary artery disease. The student, annoyed, refused to accept the reply.

"Surely, Sir, you are not saying that all of us here," the student gestured to encompass everyone in the lecture theatre, "would not be better off if we gave up drinking? Would we not be healthier, live longer and better lives?"

Hamish looked at the student sadly.

"Aye, give up whisky if you've a mind to. Give up sex, too, and animal fat and cookies and ice cream. Give up all the wee pleasures of life and go jogging every day. Maybe you will be healthier. You'll not live forever, of course, but by God it will feel like it."

Hamish is a connoisseur of whisky who knows as much about the mysteries of Scotch as he does about human anatomy. Over a dram in the Red Bar of London's fashionable Grosvenor House, he told me of his brush with the medical student, and, almost inevitably, we began talking about Scotch. We spoke not of the great blends and distinctive single malts, but of whisky's universal appeal. Why

is it, we wondered, that so many people prefer to drink Scotch whisky rather than other beverage alcohol? Why has it become popular throughout the world on a scale that no other spirit has ever matched? Cognac is drunk in most countries, so is sherry, and port, too, but their sales are no more than a fraction of the hundreds of millions of bottles of Scotch that are sold internationally each year.

Why Scotch? One reason surely is its Scottish origins. Quite apart from the legions of people round the world who claim Scottish ancestry, however distant, numberless others have an affection for Scotland, its people, its history, and its culture—and as most all Scots would agree, one cannot really understand any of these without learning to appreciate the whisky. That alone, though, would not account for the universal popularity of Scotland's national drink.

Another reason could well lie in the nature of Scotch. In an age when health has become almost an unhealthy obsession, people are attracted to Scotch because it is an entirely natural drink, made only from cereals and water and yeast and, unlike beer and wine, contains no chemicals. Calorie counters may well also be aware that Scotch contains only some sixty-six calories in a one-ounce measure, less than wine and far less than beer.

Reputation and prestige must also be factors in the appeal of Scotch whisky. It has for generations been a symbol of prosperity, associated with social prestige and professional success in many countries, and long ago surpassed champagne in popularity at diplomatic receptions in embassies everywhere.

Salesmanship, marketing, and advertising have clearly helped in promoting sales, but only to a limited extent. Brands of Scotch have been produced with a particular market in mind, blended to suit what the market researchers said would be the taste of the day and launched with a massive fanfare of Madison Avenue advertising and public relations trumpets, only to find little favour with the ultimate judges the people who drink Scotch.

If we apportion part of the credit for Scotch's universal appeal to its Scottishness, a part to its

health-giving properties, a part to its prestige, and still another to good marketing, what have we left? The answer, certainly—and this must be the most compelling reason for its worldwide success—is its flavour and character. Having said that, I must immediately correct myself; not "flavour" but "flavours". One of the great merits of Scotch is that it offers a wide range of flavours for the discerning palate, some only subtly different from others, but each with its own individual character. And just as each Scotch—blend, single malt or vatted malt—has its own individuality, so must the choice of which Scotch to drink be a matter of individual preference.

For the lover of Scotch whisky this great range of choice is the supreme attraction of the drink. You can select an obscure Scotch, let us say a

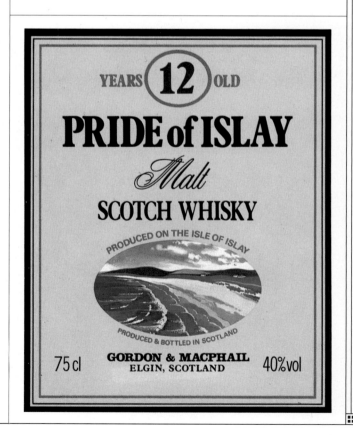

single malt from a little-known and unfashionable distillery in a remote region of the Scottish Highlands, and decide it is the finest Scotch whisky of them all. People may argue with you, but they can never prove you wrong—because you are not wrong. It is this whisky which appeals to you most and best suits your individual palate, and that is an incontrovertible fact, the ultimate truth.

As you drink your favourite Scotch whisky, you may well reflect on what gives it the inimitable flavour you enjoy. Scotland itself surely makes a vital contribution; the water, the barley, the peat—which is heather and broom and turf, pressed and concentrated for thousands of years—and the soft Scottish air in which the whisky must age.

The flavour and character of Scotch whisky are also an amalgam of many judgements. The maltster must decide how much peat to use in the malt kiln, the stillman must determine when to start and stop collecting the spirit from the second distillation, the blender must evaluate each cask of whisky to judge whether it is ready to be added to his blend, and so on. Scotch whisky is itself a blend—a blend of nature's gifts, craftsmanship, and tradition.

The ancients may well have believed that drinking Scotch was the secret of longevity. That was why they called it "uisge beatha", Gaelic for the "water of life". If my friend Hamish had thought of it, he could have put his tiresome medical student in his place with a simple quotation from James Hogg, the nineteenth century Scottish poet. Hogg was talking about whisky from the glen of the Livet, but what he said could be applied to all Scotch whisky:

If a body could just find oot the exac'
proper proportion and quantity that
ought to be drunk every day and keep
to that, I verily trow that he might leeve
for ever, without dying at a' and that
doctors and kirkyards would go oot o'
fashion.

With some regret we have to concede that not even Scotch whisky holds the secret of immortality. However, drinking it, getting acquainted with its secrets and its subtleties, learning to appreciate its unique qualities, will at least provide a lifetime of pleasure.

The Spirit of Our Ancestors

In 1891 a small firm of wine merchants in Perth High Street, founded fifty years previously by a crofter's son from the village of Aberfeldy, received a letter from an American millionaire. Andrew Carnegie was a Scot who had emigrated to the United States, made his fortune, and retired to Scotland to live the life of a Scottish gentleman. His letter read:

Cluny Castle, September 21, 1891.

Messrs John Dewar & Sons,
      Merchants,
         Perth.

Gentlemen:

      Can you get a small keg, say nine or ten gallons, of the best Scotch Whisky you can find, and ship it addressed as follows:

To the PRESIDENT,
      The Honorable Benjamin Harrison,
        Executive Mansion,
          Washington, D. C.,
            U. S. A.

Send bill to me.

      Yours Very Truly,

Andrew Carnegie

Whisky had been distilled in Scotland for hundreds of years before Carnegie ordered his gift of it for President Harrison. The art of distilling is known to have been brought to Scotland from Europe by early Christian monks, proving, so many Scots believe, that whisky, if not actually a gift from God, at least has divine approval. In medieval times spirits made in Europe mainly from grapes were named in Latin "aqua vitae", meaning "water of life". The Scots distilled barley to make their *aqua vitae* and translated the name into Gaelic as "uisge beatha", which was contracted to "uisge" and eventually to "whisky". Speaking of whisky, Holinshed in his *Chronicles*, written in the sixteenth century, claims that "it sloweth age, it strengtheneth youth, it helpeth digestion, it cutteth flegme, it abandoneth melancholie, it relisheth the heart, it lighteneth the mind, it quickeneth the spirits…" and concluded that "trulie it is a sovereigne liquor if it be orderlie taken."

Carnegie's letter was both symbolic and momentous, symbolic of the affinity between Scotland and the United States, momentous because it inspired Tom Dewar, a partner in the Perth firm of wine merchants, to start exporting his whisky around the world, and especially to the States. His move would soon be followed by other Scottish firms and would eventually lead to Americans drinking many times as much Scotch as the Scots themselves.

The main reason for the affection which so many Americans feel for Scotland is a common ancestry. Samuel Johnson, the English scholar and cynic, once remarked that the best prospect for a Scot was the road to England. It is true that many leading banks, corporations, and institutions in England are run by Scotsmen, but a far greater number of the most ambitious and enterprising Scots have gone to make their homes in more distant parts of the world, particularly in the United States, Canada, Australia, and New Zealand. Hundreds of thousands of Scots also emigrated across the Atlantic from their farms and crofts in the Western Highlands and islands when they were evicted by

Terry Purke (opposite) models the highland habit of the Appin Regiment of the Jacobite Army, the personal guard of Prince Charles Edward that fought valiantly during the Bonnie Prince's historic attempt to take the British throne in 1746. A cockade made from white satin ribbon on the cap symbolizes allegiance to Prince Charles Edward; the opposing armies wore black ones. Purke is part of an American reenactment group that tours the country, performing at Scottish festivals and Highland Games, such as this one in Roanoke, Virginia.

Perth is the home of the best known of all Scottish army regiments, the Black Watch, which gave its name to a world-famous plaid (above).

In addition to the tartan and the sword, a Highlander would also carry with him a *quaich* (previous page), the traditional vessel from which Scotch whisky was drunk. Early versions of these shallow, two-handled bowls were thought to have been made from skulls, but today they are made from silver or pewter.

Kenneth Trist Urquhart of that Ilk (opposite), the twenty-sixth hereditary chief of the Urquhart clan, was the guest of honour at Virginia's 1988 Blue Ridge Highland Games. An American from New Orleans, he succeeded his father in 1974 and assumed the title "Urquhart of that Ilk". The Urquhart clan, one of almost one hundred Scottish clans scattered throughout the world, traces its descent from the legendary warrior Conachar Mor, scion of the Royal House of Ulster, who ruled the territory around Loch Ness in ancient times. Ruins of the Urquhart Castle (below) still stand on the shores of Loch Ness.

landlords, who wished to graze sheep on the land, during the infamous "clearances" of the first half of the nineteenth century.

Proud though they are of being American or Canadian, the millions of people of Scottish ancestry—these Gordons and Grants, Macdonalds and MacLeods, Campbells and Camerons—remember their roots with affection, celebrating St. Andrew's Night and Burns Night, forming clan societies and holding Highland Games and Gatherings all over North America. To satisfy their nostalgia for Scottish lifestyles and culture, a whole network of stores and services has sprung up, boutiques selling only Highland dress and accessories, geneologists who specialize in tracing Scottish origins, schools of Highland dancing, bagpiping, and Scottish fiddling. There is even a magazine of Scottish heritage, *The Highlander*, which lists all the societies and the events they organize and publishes informative articles on Scottish history, life, and culture.

The early Celtic settlers were also the foundation of the North American whiskey industry. Deprived of the whisky that had been part of their lives at home, they soon began making their own in the New World, distilling bourbon and rye. The strong ties of blood and affection between North America and Scotland also meant there was a ready market for Scotch whisky when Tom Dewar, James Buchanan, and John Walker began to ship it across the Atlantic towards the end of the last century. By the outbreak of the First World War, the best known blends of Scotch could be found in the finer bars and restaurants and on the shelves of a growing number of liquor stores. The war, followed immediately by Prohibition, brought to an abrupt halt the enjoyment which many Americans and Canadians, not just those of Scottish origin, were finding in the flavour of Scotch, but the halt was only temporary.

Ironically, it was Prohibition that gave an immense boost to the popularity of Scotch in North America. Much of the liquor offered in speakeasies was of a most inferior quality and often dangerous to the health. Black-Strap Alky, Panther Whisky, Happy

Sally, and Yack-Yack Bourbon were only a few of the drinks with which Americans slaked their thirst. Scotch, on the other hard, when one could get it, was a drink that had been properly distilled from natural ingredients and properly matured, its quality guaranteed by the strict requirements of its legal definition in Scotland. and the watchful eyes of the Excise.

Canny Scots quickly saw the possibilities of the situation, and soon huge quantities of Scotch were being smuggled into the States, mainly from the Caribbean and over the Canadian border. Schooners would sail openly up and down the twelve-mile limit off the eastern seaboard and

transfer the cargoes of Scotch they had picked up in the Bahamas to fast motorboats sent out by bootleggers. A skipper of one schooner, Bill McCoy from Florida, earned himself not only a million dollars but a little place in the dictionaries. A man of high principle, he refused to carry any but the best brands of Scotch, and the expression "The Real McCoy" entered the English language as a synonym for quality.

In Canada, enterprising businessmen built warehouses not far north of the border in Saskatchewan, to which Americans would drive to collect cases of Scotch. What they did was not against the law and was tacitly condoned by the

Canadian government, which was glad of the export earnings. Fast cars were the most usual form of transport used by bootleggers, and the Studebaker Whisky Six, stripped of its upholstery and with reinforced springs, could carry forty cases. The only danger to the smuggler came not from customs officers—who seldom stopped them—but from other bootleggers who might try to highjack the load.

Scotch had for many years been a popular drink in Canada, which was the home of many expatriate Scots. Canadian corporations were beginning to invest in the Scotch whisky industry. Hiram Walker bought the first of the several distilleries which it was to own in Scotland in 1930, and the Seagram Company formed a joint venture with Distillers Company Limited, by far the largest whisky company in Scotland.

By the time Prohibition was repealed, the reputation of Scotch as a distinctive drink and one of the highest quality had been established. Its popularity spread rapidly throughout the States and Canada, helped by its portrayal in films and plays and novels as the chosen drink of the affluent and the fashionable. After the Second World War, the boom in foreign travel brought millions of Americans to Scotland for the first time. There, while enjoying the scenic beauty and romantic

Recent years have seen an awakening of interest in Scotch whisky, particularly the single malts, throughout the United States. Encouraged by innovative promotions like the "Whisky Passport" at Bullfeathers (below) in Washington, D. C. and schooled at whisky tastings like the one held periodically at Keen's Chop House (opposite) in New York City, many Americans are enjoying Scotch for the first time and long-time whisky lovers find themselves trying new brands in new ways.

history of the country, they also learnt about Scotch whisky; of the care and skill that goes into its making, of its many subtle flavours, of the ways in which it can be drunk and enjoyed, and of the part it plays in Scottish life and culture. This has been reflected in the changing appreciation of Americans for Scotch whisky. They have become more sophisticated in their tastes, looking for and enjoying the twelve-year-old blends and the subtle range of flavours in the single malt Scotches.

During the last decade or two, with incomes increasing and more leisure at their disposal, people have started to take a greater interest in what they eat and drink. At the same time, scores of new restaurants have sprung up, offering a wide variety of ethnic cuisines. Together, these trends encourage people to want to know how food and drinks are made, how they should best be eaten or drunk, and how they should be judged. In line with this new interest, liquor stores stock imported wines from countries which most of us never associated with vineyards, new cookery books are published almost daily, and wine writers are given prominent space in newspapers and magazines for their columns.

For Scotch whisky this has meant an awakening of interest, among women as well as men, in the different flavours that it has to offer and a swing towards the single malts and twelve-year-old, premium blends. Not very long ago I was asked to give a talk on Scotch at a club in San Jose. As the talk was to be followed by a tasting of Scotches, the sponsors decided for practical reasons to limit the audience to fifty club members. I was surprised to find that almost all of the members who turned up were obviously under thirty-five, and a good proportion of them must have been under thirty; they were mainly, I guessed, rising young business executives. What surprised me even more was their interest in single malt whiskies. As we tasted the whiskies and chatted, I found no one there who was trying a single malt for the first time. Most of the audience knew and could talk knowledgeably about

three or four. Their chief grumble was that more single malts were not available in their part of the world. Therefore they had to rely on friends visiting Scotland to bring them back a bottle or two of the malts they wished to taste.

Because of the growing interest in Scotch, many bars in the States now offer selections of single malts and blends just as extensive as those one would find in Scotland. Jake O'Shaughnessey's in Seattle has one of the largest collections, with over fifty single malts, while Arthur's Restaurant in Pittsburgh has 270 different brands of Scotch. At both places regular tastings are held for malt whisky fans, and the same is true of Keen's Chop House in New York. Dan Beck, the bar manager at Keen's, has some forty single malt Scotch whiskies on offer and holds regular tastings for customers who wish to sample and learn about malt whisky.

New York City has its own "Scotch Whisky Trail", which includes upscale, Upper East-Side bars like the Aurora, and downtown pubs like South Street Seaport's North Star, which caters to the Wall Street crowd. The unofficial nationwide whisky trail might also include The Odeon in Philadelphia, both the Stars Restaurant and the Compass Rose in San Francisco, the Heathman in Portland, Oregon, and Cutter's in Santa Monica. At Bullfeathers in the nation's capital, a patron can

apply for a "Whisky Passport", a card upon which one records every Scotch sampled. When each of the bar's forty whiskies has been tried, the by-now knowledgeable whisky connoisseur can chose a dram of his choice, on the house.

There are many more which could be added to the list. Where should one start? I will avoid imitating the Irishman who, when asked in the countryside for directions to Dublin, replied gravely, "If I were you I wouldn't start from here." Undoubtedly the best place to start your States-side whisky trail must be in New York's City Lights Bar, high above the streets of Manhattan. There, choosing from a selection of 125 Scotches, you will be able, as you sip your drink, to look out in daytime over fifty miles of America, or at night to enjoy what must surely be one of the most spectacular displays of glittering lights anywhere in the world. "Windows on the World", they call the 107th floor of the World Trade Center. Who knows? For anyone who tastes Scotch or tries a single malt there for the first time, its City Lights Bar may well open new windows of experience and enjoyment.

Even so, to appreciate Scotch whisky to the full, to understand the complexities and subtleties, one should go to its birthplace. Scotland is a tiny country, but it offers bewildering contrasts in scenery: calm, pastoral lowlands; rugged, storm-lashed islands; towering, snow-capped mountains; silent, brooding lochs; and in the extreme north a wilderness as lonely and sparsely populated as any in Europe.

As you journey through Scotland you will find the character of the land reflected in its whiskies. Lowland Malts, Highland Malts, whiskies from the islands, countless "designer" blended whiskies, together they offer a range of flavours and bouquets to intrigue the senses and delight the palate. And as you learn about the traditions of Scotch and relive its history and realize how it is inextricably a part of the Scot's life and culture, you may well conclude that Scotland is whisky and whisky is Scotland.

The Scotch Whisky Trail of New York City winds through all five boroughs, visiting glamourous nightclubs, upscale bars, neighbourhood taverns, and traditional pubs. Nestled in a booth at the North Star Pub in historic South Street Seaport (opposite), the whisky lover can have a dram beneath the towering skyscrapers of Wall Street, or perched above them all at Windows on the World on the 107th floor of the World Trade Center (above), choose from over 125 different Scotches while looking out across fifty miles of America.

The Water of Life

As the small plane carrying us from Glasgow to Islay began its descent, we could see three of the island's eight distilleries spaced along its eastern shore. Ardbeg, Lagavulin, and Laphroaig are all of them on the edge of the sea, and that morning their white buildings stood out against the brilliant blue of the water and the heather on the moors behind them.

The pilot circled the airfield suspiciously, making certain that none of the grazing sheep below him had wandered on to the single runway. One of the duties of Angus, who worked at the airfield, was to go out in a pick-up truck a few minutes before the daily plane was due to arrive and shepherd straying sheep to safety. But on Islay, time has a good deal less urgency than the Spaniard's *mañana*, and work can sometimes be overlooked in favour of other more compelling attractions—the fishing rod, a convivial dram of whisky, or even just neighbourly conversation.

Angus was working that day, and when the plane landed and had taxied up to the wooden hut which served as a terminal building, he brought out a pair of steps down which we disembarked. He was accompanied by the ground hostess, a girl of astonishing loveliness whose golden skin, dark eyes, and captivatingly haughty expression suggested that she must be from South America—Peru, perhaps, or Colombia. What magic carpet of chance, I wondered, had whisked her thousands of miles to this prosaic, peaceful

Hebridean island, to welcome passengers off a toy plane at a toy airport and, in due course no doubt, to marry a local lad and raise *bambino-bairns,* who would chatter in Spanish as fluently as they did in Gaelic? The question, through my sheer lack of inquisitiveness, remained unanswered, and Islay has many such questions.

The husband of my hostess on that visit was waiting to greet me. I knew nothing of Wishart Campbell except that a year or two previously, when they were both of an age at which many people felt they should have known better, he had married Bessie Williamson, the only woman at that time to own a distillery in Scotland. Wishart was

Canadian and formerly a professional singer, and the islanders had various theories about the magic carpet which had brought him across the Atlantic. The most romantic, though not necessarily most accurate, was that he had come to Islay searching for his great-grandfather's birthplace, met Bessie, whose heart had remained inviolate for fifty years or more, fallen instantly in love, and married her, thus becoming prince consort to the uncrowned queen of this whisky island.

In Wishart's car three golden labradors waited for us. The oldest and most senior, also named Angus, was persuaded to yield the front passenger's seat to me, though not without some good-natured

At one time all Scotch was matured in casks that had formerly held sherry. One reason for this was that sherry was shipped to Britain in casks, and rather than ship empty casks back to Spain, they were used to mature whisky. When the demand for Scotch grew so great that there were not enough sherry casks available, distillers had to look elsewhere for a source of ready-made casks and found it in the United States. There government regulations stipulate that Bourbon casks can only be used once. The type of cask affects a whisky's colour and flavour so distillers always keep track of the history of each one. The white paint on the casks at Bowmore (above) indicates a sherry cask which has previously held whisky.

The Round Church (opposite) at Bowmore was built with no corners so that the devil would have no place to hide.

❖

Previous page: Ardbeg is one of eight distilleries on Islay.

grumbling, and we set off on a quick sightseeing tour of the island before going on up "to the house" for lunch. Islay is not one of Scotland's most beautiful islands, with no savage mountains or spectacular lochs, but it is full of history. Its many standing stones are thought to have had significance in pre-Christian religions, and at one time it was invaded and colonized by Vikings and annexed to Norway. As a result, its place-names are a fascinating mixture of the Gaelic and Norse languages. Ruins of chapels on the island are thought to date back to the time of early Christian missionaries, perhaps those who brought the art of distillation from Europe to Scotland.

Wishart took me to Bowmore, one of the two small towns on Islay. There we saw a round church—built without corners so the devil would have no place to hide—and the distillery, named after the town, which stands on the edge of a sea loch whose name has always evoked a longing for home among exiled Islaymen. "Lovely Lochindaal" is how they describe it in their songs.

Bowmore was built to a plan in 1768, designed street by street and house by house, one of the earliest planned villages in Scotland. During the last war the distillery was closed and used to billet squadrons of the Royal Air Force, who flew in Catalina and Sunderland flying boats out over the ocean to guard the Atlantic convoys. One wonders how many Canadian seamen had their first treasured tastes of Islay Malt whisky smuggled out for them by their hospitable hosts from the warehouses where it lay maturing!

Beyond Bowmore, alongside a peat moss, a man stepped into the road and waved at us to stop. Wishart left the car to speak to him, and as they were talking I looked at the trench the man had cut and the rectangular chunks of peat he had stacked beside it. Peat plays an important role in the making of Scotch whisky and nowhere more so than on Islay. I had also noticed the smell of peat smoke, "peat reek", coming from the chimneys of houses which we had driven past in the villages.

When Wishart returned to the car he appeared displeased. "We've a pair of golden eagles nesting on Texa," he told me, "and that guy asked me if he might row out to the island and watch them."

Golden eagles are the pride among the many hundreds of species of birds to be found in Scotland. Islay itself is a favourite place for bird watchers, who go there to watch the Greenland barnacle geese, Greenland whitefronts, and greylags grazing in the fields near the lochs and tidal flats or wheeling overhead in huge formations. Over 250 species of birds have been recorded on the island, most of which breed there. Not too many years ago, because of the greed and stupidity of hunters, the golden eagle was in

danger of becoming extinct, together with the sea eagle and the osprey. Now rigorously protected, they are returning to add grandeur to the moors and mountains with their wonderful, soaring flight. Texa, Wishart explained, was a small uninhabited island he and Bessie owned that lay not far out at sea opposite their distillery.

"I told him no way. I don't trust that Angus," he added, implying that the other Anguses on Islay, including his dog, were to be trusted. "My hunch is that he's after either the eggs or the chicks of the eagles, both of which would get a good price if you know where to take them."

I soon discerned that Wishart mistrusted the people of Islay, not unreasonably perhaps, because they mistrusted him. All islanders are insular, and behind the natural courtesy and charm of the people of Islay one can sense a barrier of reserve and suspicion against anyone from the mainland. A man can settle on Islay, or any of the Scottish islands, and live there for forty years but still remain an "incomer". Only his children will have the right to be treated as islanders.

We drove round the island with its rapidly changing contrasts in scenery; almost treeless desolation on the west, farmhouses and neatly cultivated fields in the centre, rugged hills and cliffs in the extreme south, and, along the southeast, sheltered from the Atlantic gales, woodland where one can even find a palm tree or two.

After stopping to look at the High Cross in Kildalton, which dates back to about 800 A.D. and is considered the finest Celtic cross in Scotland,

Laphroaig, pronounced "La-Froyg", is an all-malt Scotch whisky from the remote island of Islay in the Western Isles of Scotland Laphroaig is a Gaelic word, and means "the beautiful hollow by the broad bay".

In the making of Laphroaig, malted barley is dried over a peat fire. The smoke from this peat, found only on the island of Islay, gives Laphroaig its particularly rich flavour.

Laphroaig is best savoured neat, or with a little cool water.

Deerstalking is an ancient and traditional sport on the islands and in the Highlands, and a useful one, too, since it helps to control the deer population. Deerstalker Carol Harris (opposite) comes to the Western Highlands from Oxford.

❖

Previous pages: The High Cross at Kildalton (page 38), the oldest standing cross in Scotland, dates back to the ninth century.

Farmers share a dram after cutting peat on a mild day (page 39).

Dark peat-smoke, shown coming from the pagodas of Bowmore Distillery (pages 40–41), fills the town with a tangy smell.

we were returning towards Laphroaig Distillery when without warning Wishart stopped the car in the middle of a dirt road. and looked at his watch.

"Past twelve. Time for the first dram."

From the glove compartment of the car he took two small silver mugs and two half-bottles of whisky, one empty and the other containing Laphroaig single malt whisky. A small trickling burn flowed by the road, and, leaving the car, Wishart filled the empty bottle from it. The water seemed clear enough, with only the faintest tint of peaty amber. Pouring whisky into each silver mug, a generous measure for me, no more than a suspicion for himself as he was driving, he added an equal amount of burn water and handed a mug to me.

"*Slainte.*" The old Gaelic toast of good health sounded strange in his Canadian accent.

I raised my mug to my lips without enthusiasm. Laphroaig had always trailed behind my favourites among single malts, its heavy, smoky flavour too pungent for my palate. Many people say they find in it an almost medicinal taste, not unlike that of iodine perhaps, and in my experience whisky drinkers either dislike Laphroaig or yearn for it with a lover's unreasoning passion.

Steeling myself to restrain the instinctive grimace which might follow the first sip, I drank and was astounded. This was a million fathoms from any Laphroaig I had ever tasted before; smoky, yes, and rich, but delightfully smooth with an authentic tang of the sea and none the worse for that.

We lunched with Bessie in their house which overlooked the distillery and the sea beyond, and she told me how she had become a whisky distiller. When she was little more than a girl teaching school in Glasgow, her father had persuaded her to come and work for his old friend Ian Hunter, who owned Laphroaig Distillery. Hunter, a difficult man in many ways, was having trouble finding anyone to help him with the office work and administration of the

distillery. Bessie agreed to come over to Islay and help him out, but only for a year. Before the year elapsed, however, Hunter had fallen ill, so Bessie then began relaying instructions from his sickbed to the men working in the maltings, on the mash tuns and washbacks and stills. Before long she had learnt all there was to know about managing the distillery, which she did so competently that when he died Hunter left her Laphroaig. Now, I already knew, she had a place in what was almost entirely a male preserve and was accepted and respected by other distillers.

"I came for a year," she said laughing, "and I've been here for almost all my life."

Disarmed by her friendliness, and a second glass of whisky, I grew bold enough to tell Bessie how different it was to any Laphroaig I had tasted before and asked her whether she was keeping a supply of her very finest whisky for her own use, in the way that directors of port wine companies are reputed to hold back special vintages for themselves.

She laughed at the accusation and assured me I was drinking the same Laphroaig that she exported all over the world. "It tastes different to you," she explained, "because the water you are adding to it is the water which we use in making the whisky down at the distillery."

Like the great majority of Scotsmen, I usually drink whisky with an equal amount of plain water, and more often than not it has been water from the tap in cities all over the world—Tokyo, Paris, Hamburg, New York, Copenhagen, Bangkok.

Bessie reproved me gently. Chemicals are added to city water, she explained, to ensure that it is safe and hygienic. Almost always these chemicals ruin the flavour of a good Scotch if the water is added to it. Whenever possible I should use a good-quality bottled water to add to my Laphroaig. That would make a world of difference.

We began to talk about water, which I knew was an extremely influential factor in determining the flavour of Scotch whisky. Every distillery in Scotland has its own source of water for distilling, usually a spring or a burn in the hills, jealously guarded and protected. Bessie told me a story that illustrates how important water could be.

The whisky distilled at Laphroaig, she told me, as well as being sold as a single malt, is widely used in blending. Because of its special character, there are at least a few drops of Laphroaig in all the finest blended Scotches. Many years previously Hunter, the owner of the distillery, used a Glasgow businessman as his agent to sell Laphroaig to the blending companies on the mainland. The agent owned a distillery of his own, and after a time, Hunter decided that he was not putting enough effort into selling Laphroaig, so he withdrew the agency. In a fury the Glasgow businessman swore that he would have his revenge on Hunter. He would build another distillery only a short distance away from Laphroaig, equip it with pot stills that were identical in shape and size to those used at Laphroaig, and copy all the processes exactly. In that way he would produce, so he thought, a whisky which would taste the same as Laphroaig and, by selling it to the blending firms on the mainland, destroy Hunter's business.

The Glasgow businessman carried out his plan and built his distillery, but when the first spirit flowed from the pot stills, although it was good whisky, an authentic Islay Malt, it was totally unlike Laphroaig in flavour. So the new distillery failed to make an impact on the sales and success of Laphroaig, and after a time, it quietly closed.

"The explanation, of course," Bessie said, "was the water. He was drawing from the same hills for his distillery, but not from our spring."

After lunch I persuaded her to show me round the distillery. She had not offered before because, as she said, I had toured many distilleries, and one is much like another, but I insisted. Distillers are proud of their craft and take pleasure in showing visitors how they make their whisky and why it is as fine as any other, if not finer. In any case, I wished to find out why malt whisky distilled on Islay was so different from that made in the Highlands and Lowlands of Scotland. Each of the eight distilleries on the island makes a whisky with a distinctive flavour, but in all of them one can detect a unique tang that is difficult to describe but which I always associate with the sea, with the saltiness of spray flung in one's face when a wave breaks on the sea wall, with green seaweed lying around silent rock pools, with fishermen's nets drying on the sand.

Malting is the first step in making whisky. In the traditional floor-malting process, barley is soaked in water and then spread out on the floor and allowed to germinate. As it lies there, it will be regularly turned with large wooden shovels known as "shiels". After several days, the germinated barley (above) will be dried in a kiln (opposite page) over a fire fuelled first with peat and then with coke or anthracite. It is the peat which gives whisky its smoky flavour. Because of the great demand for Scotch whisky today, most malt is now made in large, mechanical maltings, which can supply a number of distilleries. Balvenie is one of the few distilleries which still has its own floor maltings (right).

❖

Previous pages: The rushing Crombie (page 44) is a tributary of the Livet.

Steam rises over the sea at Islay's Bruichladdich Distillery (page 46). After the alcohol is separated from water in the still, the hot water, which is free of chemicals or toxins, is discharged.

❖

Following pages: The three mountains known as the Paps of Jura (page 51) loom across the channel from Islay's Port Askaig (page 53).

Laphroaig was at that time one of a declining number of distilleries in Scotland which made its own malt by the traditional floor-malting process. Barley is soaked in water and then spread over a stone floor where it begins to germinate, producing starch to feed the growing plant. As it lies on the floor, the sprouting grain is regularly turned by men using large, flat, wooden shovels. The turning controls the rate of germination and prevents the rootlets from becoming matted together. When germination has progressed far enough, the barley is taken to the malt kiln, spread thickly over a wire mesh floor, and dried by the heat from a fire underneath it.

Bessie led me down to the kiln and, opening the doors, pointed to the peat burning in the fire. Its smoke, going up through the wire mesh floor, impregnated the grain as it dried it. Peat is only used in the first stage of the process, the drying being finished with some form of smokeless, solid fuel. The length of time for which the peat is burned will determine the "smokiness" of the whisky. In some distilleries no peat is used at all, but Islay Malt whiskies are traditionally heavy and smoky, with Laphroaig generally considered to be the smokiest of them all.

Earlier in our tour, as we passed the loft in which the barley was stored before being malted, I had picked up a handful of it, and now I took a few grains of the dried malt as it was being taken out of the kiln. Biting into a grain of each, I decided that my theory about Islay was confirmed. The difference in taste was astonishing. The ordinary taste of malt which I expected to find in the malted barley, the taste one finds in malted milk and malt toffee, was almost overwhelmed by the flavour I always associated with Islay whisky, unmistakable even then.

That evening friends were invited by Bessie for coffee and a dram in honour of my visit. Among them were three distillers, George Ballingall, Evan Cattanach and Grant Carmichael, all with their wives. The three of them worked in distilleries owned by the Distillers Company Ltd., a company whose blended Scotches—Johnnie Walker Red and Black, Dewar's, and White Horse—are known the world over. In a sense, being distillers they were Bessie's rivals, but the realities of commercial competition seemed curiously remote on Islay.

Inevitably, as on all the Western Isles of Scotland, conversation became merged almost imperceptibly with music. Evan, with his fine tenor voice, had won medals at the Mod, the annual festival of Gaelic music which is held in a different part of Scotland each year, and he sang for us. So did Mairi, the wife of Grant Carmichael, a local girl and a Gaelic speaker whose prettiness and sweet, natural voice seemed to fill the island songs like "Westering Home" and "The Lights of Lochindaal" with a touching nostalgia.

Softened by whisky and music and the discovery of new friendships, suspicion and reserve disappeared. Even Wishart, who—he assured me and everyone agreed—no longer sang, could not resist and went finally to his white grand piano to play and sing for us the favourite light operettas and musical comedies of a decade or more ago. Such was our mood that they seemed in no way incongruous, and we joined in the choruses, growing more maudlin as the evening stretched past midnight. Below our facade of caution and canniness, we Scots are a sentimental lot.

Next morning George Ballingall collected me and drove me across the island to Caol Ila, one of his company's distilleries, named in Gaelic after the slender strip of water which separates Islay from the neighbouring island of Jura, which it overlooks. The distillery is on the very edge of the sound and around it, on the cliffs above, are clustered the houses of the men who work in it, making Caol Ila a small community, a feature typical of all the distilleries on Islay. The distillery draws its water supply from Loch nam Ban, over which Alfred Barnard, a Londoner who toured the distilleries more than one hundred years ago, wrote "ever and anon the fragrant breeze from myrtle and blooming heather is wafted".

That morning in the sunshine and the clear soft air which one finds in the west of Scotland, we had a fine view of Jura, its three mountains, the Paps of Jura, rising steeply from a narrow string of arable land around its coast and forests of conifers on their lower slopes. Grant Carmichael, the manager of Caol Ila, had a pair of binoculars in his office and with them we scanned the mountains, looking for red deer. Jura supports only about two hundred people but several thousand deer, and its name is derived from the Norse *Dyr Oe,* which means "Deer Island".

George Ballingall had arranged to meet two whisky men on Jura that morning, and he invited me to go with him. We walked over the cliffs the short distance to Port Askaig, a port in name only, with no more than a rusty landing stage flanked by a small hotel, a post office, and a petrol pump, and found Archie McPhee. At that time the only way of crossing the sound from Islay to Jura was in Archie's boat. He took us over, and on the opposite shore we were met by a friend of George who drove us the several miles along the island's only road to its only town, Craighouse, where alongside the harbour, the one hotel, the school, and the store, a new distillery had recently been built.

When we reached the distillery, George went to the office to meet his whisky friends, leaving me to stroll through Craighouse. The town has little to offer a visitor, but in the churchyard I found the grave of Gillouir MacCrain, who had been 108 years old when he died in 1645. I was told later that in a graveyard a short distance away lay

another member of that family, Mary MacCrain, who lived to 126. The islanders attribute this extraordinary longevity to the whisky made in their distillery, and when it went out of production early in this century, killed by the competition of distilleries on Islay and the mainland, they had resigned themselves to shorter and thirstier lives. They were rescued from this depressing prospect by two local landowners who persuaded an Edinburgh whisky firm to join them in building a new distillery on the site of the old one.

Had I time that morning I would have liked to make my way to the northern tip of Jura to see the notorious Gulf of Corrievreckan, where a tide race of ten knots makes a roar that can be heard twenty miles away. Many ships have foundered there. Legend says that the witch Caillich watches over the whirlpool, deciding which of the ships passing that way will be wrecked. I might also have gone to see the farmhouse in which George Orwell wrote his famous book *Nineteen Eighty-four*.

As it was I had barely walked the full length of the one street of Craighouse and back when George came out of the distillery with his two business friends. He introduced them as Donald Mackinlay and Delmé Evans. Together we went to the hotel and, as the day was fine and warm, sat in its small garden overlooking the harbour. A lassie brought us out a bottle of Scotch, a jug of water, and glasses, and I saw that the name on the label of the whisky bottle was also Mackinlay.

"This can't be a coincidence," I said to Donald, pointing at the label.

They told me it was not a coincidence. The whisky firm of Charles Mackinlay and Company had been founded by Donald's ancestors, and he was the fifth generation in direct descent from father to son to be the company's whisky blender.

"I'm surprised the hotel didn't insist on us drinking the whisky from across the way," I said, pointing toward the distillery.

"The whisky they distill is not ready to be drunk yet," Delmé Evans replied.

By law whisky made in Scotland is not entitled to the designation "Scotch whisky" until it has matured for a minimum of three years, and most Scotches are matured for longer than that. The Isle of Jura Distillery, Delmé Evans told me, had been built only four years previously, and it was not intended that its whisky should be bottled and sold until it was ten years old.

Delmé himself was an interesting character; a Welshman who farmed in a considerable way, piloted his own plane, and yet found time to build the distillery on Jura. He was planning to build another for Donald's company on Speyside. Choosing a site for a new distillery requires judgement and experience, for not even an expert can know how good the whisky will be until the first drops flow from the stills.

"Building a distillery must be something of a gamble," I remarked to Delmé.

"It wasn't in Jura. There had been a distillery on the site for many years, and its whisky had a good reputation in the old days. So we knew the water must be all right."

"What kind of water does one need?"

"There's an old saying in the trade that it should be soft water, flowing over granite and through peat."

After lunch, Delmé and Donald, who were staying on the island, drove us back to the point where we were to meet Archie McPhee. We saw no sign of him, and George said it was our visit to Jura which, like all trips to Jura, had been something of a gamble. Archie would take you across the sound, but you could never be sure that he would come to take you back. In the intervening hours he might, on reflection, decide that he did not care much for you. Alternatively, he might find, either in the bar of the Port Askaig hotel or elsewhere, a diversion which appealed to him more than boating. Or he might simply forget.

After about half-an-hour we began resigning ourselves to spending the night on Jura, and, with a mainlander's time-disciplined mind, I brooded over the inconvenience that this would cause, although in truth it would cause very little. Then his boat appeared, chugging up the sound from the south. When he reached us he said nothing, offered no apologies. I formed the impression Archie was only amused by my impatience, and on the way back to Port Askaig he glanced at me with a sardonic smile that was no more than a twitch of the lips. Then, ostentatiously, he began humming "Westering Home", the song of the exile returning to Islay.

… Laughter of love and a welcoming there,
Isle of my heart, my own one.

Skye, the most beautiful of the islands of Scotland, was the inspiration for another song, also full of nostalgia, not for the island but for a folk hero.

Speed, bonnie boat, like a bird on the wing,
Onward, the sailors cry:
Carry the lad that's born to be king,
Over the sea to Skye.

Although he never achieved his birthright, Prince Charles Edward, Bonnie Prince Charlie, was the lad born to be king. To understand his appeal to the Scots, one must know something of Scotland's history. James II, King of Scotland and England, was deposed by the English and forced to flee into exile. The great majority of Scots believed, and many believe to this day, that James and his successors remained the rightful kings.

Prince Charles, the grandson of James, was born in Rome. In 1745, at the age of twenty-five, he landed in Inverness with seven companions determined to recapture his throne. Within a short time more than two thousand Scots had rushed to join his army, and he made a daring march on England, defeating English armies on the way. He was only 120 miles from London and might well have captured the capital and retaken the throne, but his generals took fright and persuaded him to withdraw. His retreat to Scotland became a rout and finally ended at Culloden, where his troops were annihilated by an army led by the Duke of Cumberland. He and his followers were hunted down with savage brutality by the English and after months as a fugitive, Charles fled to Skye. Eventually he escaped from the island and returned to Rome where, deprived of his birthright and of Scotch whisky, he died, some say of a broken heart and others say from drinking Italian brandy.

Culloden, the last battle to be fought on the soil of Britain, destroyed Scottish independence. "Freedom and Whisky gang thegither", wrote Robert Burns, and, as history was later to show, the Scots were fighting for their whisky as much as for their freedom. From the earliest times every Scot was free to make his own whisky, and though an Excise Duty on whisky had been passed in 1644, no serious attempts had been made to collect it outside the cities in the south. The battle of Culloden opened up the Highlands; roads were built and along them came the Excise Officers, collecting the tax on whisky.

It was not far from the mournful battlefield at Culloden that, some years after my first visit to Islay, I met, at the Tulchan Lodge hotel, three highlanders who by their appearance seemed almost to have survived the 240 years since the battle. They were all in the whisky business: Michael Thomson from the firm of Peter Thomson of Perth, which produces Beneagles whisky; Sandy Gordon from William Grant and Sons; John Grant, whose family owns Glenfarclas Distillery in the valley of the Spey.

All three were on their way to start an expedition into the past which Michael had organized,

retracing the steps of Prince Charles Edward on his escape across the Highlands. What made the expedition unique and challenging was that they would dress as closely as possible to the way clansmen did at that time and try to live off the land, eating only animals or fish that they could hunt. The only food they would carry would be a quantity of oatmeal and a bottle of whisky each. In the elegance of Tulchan Lodge they looked out of place, like eighteenth century fugitives, wearing not the tailored kilts of today but the traditional *feiladh mor* plaid, a length of tartan cloth some sixteen feet long and five feet wide, which would protect them against the weather and serve as a sleeping bag.

Not long afterwards I made my own way to Skye, but travelling in comfort by car to Mallaig on the west coast and then by ferry to Armdale on the southern tip of the island. I quite enjoy driving in

Prince Charles Edward, better known as Bonnie Prince Charlie, was the grandson of the deposed British king. He tried to take the throne at the age of twenty-five, but was defeated on the battlefield at Culloden (above) in 1746. He fled to Skye (overleaf), and from there into exile.

The Battle of Culloden was also important in the history of Scotch whisky. After defeating Prince Charles Edward, the British, determined to subjugate the unruly Scottish clans, moved troops into the area. Gradually the once-remote Highlands—and Highland Malts—became accessible to the world.

Scotland. Apart from the central region around Glasgow and Edinburgh, the countryside has not been ravaged by long, growling strips of motorway, and the main roads are good and not crowded, except during the holiday months of July and August. The greatest pleasure, though, is to turn off the main roads into the lanes which twist, turn, and dip, giving sudden and unexpected views of dazzling beauty. And such is the friendliness of the Highland Scot that any motorist in trouble will soon find someone who will be glad to help him.

Skye—in Gaelic *Eilean a' Cheo*, the "isle of mist"—is not an island but an intoxication, firing the senses with its beauty, its history, and its charm. Above the tranquil loneliness of the sea loch which cuts into its shore stands the most majestic mountain range in Scotland, the Cuillins, witnesses through the ages to countless bloody battles between the Macdonalds and the MacLeods.

The two clans fought for land and dominance, but never matched the pervasive power over the islanders held by a third, less visible group of inhabitants, the *Sithe*, or fairies. Even now their influence lingers in fairy bridges and fairy banners with magical powers, and every village, every hill, every burn, almost every rock has its own superstition of a fairy gift or a fairy curse.

For those who seek romance, the fugitive path through Skye of Bonnie Prince Charlie can be traced in caves where he hid, burns which he forded, beaches on which he landed. The epitaph for Charles Edward's adventure is the grave of Flora Macdonald, who helped him escape when he was being hunted by the English on Skye by disguising him as her serving maid. For that she was arrested by the English and imprisoned. Although her case had made her a celebrity in London, when she was pardoned she married and moved to the United States. Eventually, however, she returned to Skye and died there.

Skye also has a distillery, Talisker, and late in the evening after arriving on the island, I tasted its malt whisky. Connoisseurs of whisky say that they find a distinctive flavour in all island whiskies, that same tang of the sea so noticeable in Islay Malts, which may be partly disguised by other characteristics but is always there. Wishing to put this theory to the test, in the bar of my hotel I ordered two island whiskies, Talisker from Skye and Highland Park from the Orkneys, set them on the counter in front of me, and tasted them in turn. Both were classic malt whiskies, both peaty and each with a distinctive taste of its own. Talisker seemed the drier of the two, slightly astringent, while Highland Park was robust and sweeter. I was almost certain that I could detect the "island" character in both.

A man standing not far from me in the bar was watching me as I sipped from each of my two glasses in turn. He seemed amused, so I explained what I was attempting to do.

"Highland Park and Talisker?" he said. "Aye, they're both island whiskies, the same as Laphroaig. No doubt about that."

"But there is a difference, in their island character I mean."

"Surely. In Laphroaig the taste explodes on one's palate, in Highland Park it's the grumble of a cello in a string quartet." He paused. "Now in Talisker it creeps up on you like a *haar*."

A *haar*, I knew, was a soft pervasive sea mist so typical of the west of Scotland, and on the misty isle his analogy was perfect. "Are you in the whisky business?" I asked him.

"No, I work in a garage in Portree, and I've a croft as well."

We chatted for a while, not about whisky but about life on the islands of Scotland. At one time Skye had been almost entirely farmed by crofters with five to ten-acre plots of land and common grazing, but as with the other Western Isles thousands of crofters had been evicted in the notorious clearances to make way for sheep. Today most crofters work at other occupations, and financial support from the European Economic Community and tourism have restored a measure of prosperity to the island.

By contrast, the Orkney Islands to the north of Scotland are far more fertile and have attracted settlers for thousands of years. For this reason they are rich in historical interest. Scara Brae, the well preserved site of a prehistoric village, dates back four thousand years to neolithic times. In many ways the Orkneys are the least Scottish of

The peaty Talisker is distilled on Skye. Derek Bottomer (opposite), the manager of Talisker, has a dram while looking out over Loch Harport.

❖

Previous pages: Peat is moist when it is cut (page 59) and must be dried before it can be burned as fuel.

The countryside of Skye is dotted with crofts (page 60), the inhabitants of which feel a strong loyalty to the locally-produced whisky.

Scotland's islands; colonized by Vikings for several hundred years, they only came under Scottish rule in the fifteenth century.

We were still talking late into the night when we heard that the Skye Mountain Rescue Team had been called out earlier in the evening. The team is a band of volunteers, drawn from all trades and professions, who rescue climbers in trouble on the mountains. Drawn by a writer's curiosity I drove to the inn at Sligachan, which a hundred years ago was one Europe's leading climbing centres: Victorian gentlemen came there to scale the peaks while their wives painted, trying to improve on Turner's romanticized portrayal of Loch Coruisk's stern grandeur.

By the time I reached the inn, the members of the rescue team had already returned, satisfied that their mission had been accomplished safely and speedily. Often they would be on the mountains all night and even longer, searching for climbers who had gone out ill-prepared, ignoring advice and placing their own lives and those of others in danger. That night the rescue had, for once, been comparatively simple. The visitors had been climbing, properly equipped, in a party of three, when one of them was injured by falling rock. One of his companions had stayed with him while the other went for help.

The injured climber had been brought down, without recourse to a helicopter from the mainland, and taken to hospital, and now the rescue team were relaxing over a dram in the inn. Among those whom I met was Derek Bottomer, the manager of Talisker Distillery. When he heard of my interest in whisky, he invited me to visit the distillery the following morning.

Talisker is situated above Loch Harport, separated from the sea loch by a road which runs through the village of Carbost. When the distillery was built in 1830, the minister of the parish said it was "one of the greatest curses that, in the ordinary course of Providence, could befall it or any other place". Instead it has brought regular work in an ancient and satisfying craft to successive generations of Skyemen and produces a Scotch whisky that is known and valued all over the world.

Derek Bottomer proved to be an interesting and likeable man, and a lover of the mountains which form a backdrop to his distillery. Daffodils were growing in the garden of his house nearby, but snow still lay on the peaks of the Cuillins. The weather had been unusually fine for several days, and Derek told me that he and his wife had spent eleven hours walking on the hills the previous Sunday.

By then I had formed a theory about island whiskies, which was that their distinctive flavour came from the smoke of the peat burned in the malt kiln. Any island is washed continually by sea spray or shrouded in sea mist, and in this way becomes imbued with that medicinal, iodine flavour of the sea. Islay, which was comparatively flat, would be far more exposed to these elements than either Jura or Skye, on which the peat mosses would be partly sheltered from sea spray by mountains. This greater exposure to the elements would explain the much stronger island flavour of Islay Malts. When I told Derek my theory, he listened courteously.

"Peat can't be the reason for that flavour in Talisker whisky," he said.

"Why not?"

"Because we bring in our malted barley from the mainland."

Until a few years ago the distillery had its own maltings, but the whisky blenders who owned it also owned several other distilleries in Scotland and now malt for all of them was made in three centralized locations on the mainland. There, as Derek pointed out, local sources of peat and not island peat would be burned in the kilns.

"In a sense your theory could still be right," he said.

He took me into the distillery and showed me the mash tun, a large circular vessel in which the malted barley, after being ground into grist, was mixed with water. It is here that the soluble starch is extracted from the grain, making a sugary liquid which is then cooled, fermented, and distilled into spirit.

The water used for mashing at Talisker comes from the Carbost burn which flows down Snoc nan Speireag, "the hill of the hawk". One can see just by looking at it that it is peaty. Much of the water

in the springs and burns of Scotland is peaty enough to have a faint brown tint, which turns much browner at times of heavy rain. So it may well be the island peat which gives Talisker malt whisky its flavour, but through the water and not in the malt kiln.

Derek was probably being kind, not wishing to hurt my feelings, but my disappointment at learning that my theory was wrong soon passed. The lesson to be learned, I told myself, was that water was the single most important factor in the making of Scotch whisky. Was that why the ancient Scots called it "uisge beatha", which means "the water of life"?

Glenmorangie Distillery stands just outside the small town of Tain, and if, driving there from Skye, one scorns the shortest route and loops round to the north, one passes through what many would argue is the most beautiful part of Scotland. The Trossachs, not far north of Glasgow, have a peaceful, time-enduring loveliness, so has Loch Lomond, so have the lochs and glens of the Cairngorms, and so has Deeside. But in splendour Wester Ross has no rival, with its great silent lochs, brooding mountain ranges, and spectacular waterfalls in a wilderness of nature on a scale unmatched anywhere in Britain. The roads belong to another age, twisting and absurdly narrow as they wind precariously over Applecross peninsula, past Loch Torridon with its magnificent backcloth of mountains—Beinn Eighe, Liathach, and the

jewelled mountain, Beinn Alligin—to lovely Loch Maree. Then at the end of the day, if you look back the way you came, you may well see a splendour which beggars superlatives, the sight of the sun sinking beyond the Cuillins of Skye into the vast loneliness of the Atlantic.

At Glenmorangie I was shown round the distillery by George Thomson, a refugee from city life. George used to work in a whisky research laboratory in Edinburgh until he saw an advertisement for the post of assistant manager at Glenmorangie. In Edinburgh he had to drive to work every morning across the city and face the return journey in the evening. Now he saunters a hundred yards or less to work from his home in the distillery grounds, and, as he says, instead of analysing and calculating and peering into the sterile screen of a computer, he is one of a creative team using their skill, knowledge, patience, and care to make a product for which Scotland is rightly famous, a fine whisky.

Malt whiskies of Scotland are generally divided into classes according to the region in which they are distilled: Highland Malts, from anywhere north of an imaginary line from Greenock in the west to Dundee in the east; Lowland Malts, made south of that line; Islay Malts, from the island of Islay; and Campbeltown Malts, from the Mull of Kintyre. Highland Malts are often divided into two categories: Speyside malts—distilled in or near the valley of the River Spey—and others.

Glenmorangie, a name often mispronounced—remember orange, they tell you at the distillery, and you will say it right—is thus an "other" Highland Malt, as are Talisker and Highland Park. Elegant and delicate are two adjectives which always spring to my mind when I sip Glenmorangie, for it has only a light smokiness and no hint at all of sweetness, perhaps because it is never matured in sherry casks.

Alice Ross lives in a small cottage in Glenmorangie Distillery, near enough to the cooperage for her to hear the hammering

In this copper mash tun at Bowmore (page 65), the crushed malt mixes with water. This process releases the sugar, which will be converted into alcohol. After several hours in the mash tun, the liquid is drained off to the washback (opposite); the "draff", which is left behind, is sold to farmers for use as animal feed. In the washback, yeast is added to the liquid and immediately fermentation begins. When fermentation is complete, usually in a few days, the wort, as the liquid is now called, is pumped into the pot still (page 69). There the liquid is boiled, and since alcohol boils at a lower temperature than water, the alcohol vapours rise to the neck of the still and condense in copper pipes.

❖

Following page: Distillery workers at Talisker on Skye gather for a break in the morning sunshine.

of the coopers as they reassemble or repair the American oak casks in which the whisky will mature. Her father had been head cooper at the distillery, working there an almost unbelievable seventy years, and since Alice is nearer ninety than eighty, together they have seen literally millions of gallons of Glenmorangie single malt whisky leave the distillery, bringing pleasure to connoisseurs of malt whisky everywhere. Like all true Scots, Alice is sturdily independent and that is why she still insists on going over to the distillery at seven every morning to clean the offices. The story of Alice and her father is by no means unique. Making Scotch whisky has always been a family business, a craft handed down from one generation to the next.

As George took me round the distillery and I saw the washbacks, large circular vessels in which yeast is added to the liquid produced in the mash tun and fermentation takes place, I noticed that they were made of stainless steel. At Talisker they had been made of wood, spruce, I thought, or perhaps larch. When I asked George the reason

for using steel, he told me it was more practical. Washbacks must be cleaned after each fermentation, and cleaning wooden washbacks is a long and laborious business. Steel washbacks, he said, were more hygienic and made it easier to control the quality of the wash and, therefore, the whisky.

"Then what gives Glenmorangie its special character?" I asked George.

"I'll show you one reason."

Scotch malt whisky is distilled twice in traditional copper pot stills. The stills at Glenmorangie are tall and slender. At almost seventeen feet high, they are the tallest pot stills in Scotland, and this towering height, the company believe, ensures that only the purest vapours are captured and condensed into spirit.

"Another reason is the water." George said. "Our water comes from a spring on Tarlogie Hill, only half-a-mile or so from here."

"A beautiful soft water, I suppose, flowing over granite through peat?"

"Not at all. A hard water rich in minerals from the red sandstone of Ross."

I looked at him incredulously. I did not know then that this was the beginning of another lesson. For every opinion you will hear expressed by a whisky man in Scotland, you may well hear a diametrically opposite view expressed with equal conviction and sincerity. That does not mean distillers are perverse, simply that there is so much about the making of Scotch that not even they fully understand.

The Whisky Trail—Speyside

The land around the Spey, one of the famous salmon rivers of Scotland, is sleepy and peaceful, unexpectedly so for the Highlands. Its undulating contours present a sharp contrast to the Grampian and Cairngorm Mountains to the south and the rugged wilderness north of Inverness. Drive along the main road from Grantown to Elgin and you will see few signs of bustling activity. But you will see whisky distilleries, mostly by the river or up on the heather-clad hills. Each is a small cluster of white buildings often recognizable by the pagoda chimneys of the malt kilns, even though few of them make their own malt anymore. Their names will bring a nostalgic longing to single malt whisky buffs everywhere: Glenlivet, Glenfarclas, Tormore, Knockando, Cardhu, Macallan, Glen Grant, Milton Duff, Linkwood, and Longmorn. Stray a mile or two from the main road and you will find more; Glenfiddich, Mortlach and Balvenie in Dufftown, Strathisla and Strathmill in Keith.

The Fiddichside Inn must be the smallest inn in Scotland. You will find it just outside the village of Craigellachie, perched on the banks of the Fiddich not far from where it flows into the Spey. Anglers go to the inn in the evenings to relive—or drown—the memory of a day with the rod and find themselves mingling in the tiny bar with distillers, not surprisingly for this is malt whisky country. Salmon fishing aside, the valley of the Spey is

Scotland's golden triangle, its forty-two distilleries making it the richest part of the country, earning more than the steel mills and shipyards of Glasgow, more than the silicon chips of the New Towns in the central belt of Scotland.

Dorothy Brandie owns the Fiddichside Inn, but one should not be deceived by her name. She knows her whiskies, and she knows her whisky distillers. Mention a name to her and more often than not she will tell you that she knows the man and knew his father as well, for distilling is a tradition in this part of Scotland, a craft handed down from father to son. Dorothy certainly belongs to the tradition, for even though she does not make malt whisky, but only sells it, her grandfather had a reputation for distilling the finest in the Highlands, secretly and in defiance of the law.

An old, faded photograph of him hangs on the wall of the bar in the Fiddichside Inn. James Smith of Glass, universally known as Goshen, was one of hundreds of smugglers–moonshiners would be a better name–who for more than 250 years after the Scottish Excise Bill was passed in 1644 refused to pay tax on whisky. All over the Highlands "bothy" stills were set up in wooded glens or on heather-covered hills, and the smugglers showed extraordinary ingenuity in camouflaging what they were doing from the hated Excise Officers–the "gaugers", they called them.

Illicit distilling was not confined to the countryside. The clock tower which stands in the centre of Dufftown once concealed an illicit still. Magnus Eunson, a preacher in the United Presbyterian Church in Orkney, had his illicit bothy on the site where Highland Park Distillery was later built, and stored the whisky he made under his pulpit. The smugglers were usually helped by their wives, both in distilling the whisky and smuggling it to markets in the south of Scotland, where it was held to be of a better quality than the whisky made in the commercial distilleries of that area. Thousands of gallons were transported there, hidden in vessels beneath the ample skirts of that time.

The double locks on distillery warehouses (below) are symbols of the continuing power of the Excise. One lock belongs to the distiller and the other to the Excise Officer, and neither can touch the whisky unless the other is present. Belly flasks and "dogs" (opposite) were well-known tools of the illicit distiller. The aptly-named belly flasks fit snuggly against the body, while the dogs were used for nipping illegal drams from casks.

Under British law the mere possession of illegal equipment is evidence enough for a conviction. There is a story of a Glasgow man who was caught making whisky in his kitchen. During the trial the arresting officer was asked if he had actually caught the man making whisky. The officer replied that he had not, but that the suspect had all the necessary equipment. In accordance with British legal tradition, before passing sentence the Sheriff asked the man if there were any other offences which he had committed that should be taken into consideration. The man thought for a few moments. "Only one, your Honour," he said, "rape." "What!" exclaimed the Sheriff. "You've committed rape?" "No, your Honour," the man replied, "but I have all the necessary equipment."

By the beginning of the nineteenth century smuggling was undermining the whole moral fabric of the Highlands of Scotland. No one considered it a crime to make whisky. Excise Officers were bribed or, if they remained incorruptible, attacked and sometimes murdered by gangs of smugglers. Sympathetic magistrates imposed no more than token fines on offenders, and thousands of otherwise honest Scots became involved in or condoned the breaking of the law.

Appalled by the widespread contempt for the law, the great landowners of the region finally decided that something must be done. In 1820 the Duke of Gordon, laird of Glenlivet, raised the matter in the House of Lords. His proposal, that legal distilling should be sanctioned on payment of a modest licence fee and the Excise Duty reduced, was incorporated in an Act of Parliament, which marked the beginning of a decline in illicit distilling and provided the foundation for the modern whisky industry.

Illicit distilling and smuggling continued after the 1823 Act and well into the twentieth century, but on a far smaller scale. Goshen was one of those who continued to defy the law, and he won an unrivalled reputation for his whisky and the generosity with which he dispensed drams to his friends and neighbours. In the end he was betrayed to the authorities, unluckily and in bizarre circumstances.

Sir William Grant, a man well-known in public life, sampled Goshen's whisky while on holiday on Speyside and later boasted of its quality in an after-dinner speech which he made in London. Unaware that one of his fellow guests was a senior official in the Excise, Grant gave away enough information in casual conversation for Goshen to be identified. Goshen's bothy was raided, and only the eloquence of his lawyer in court saved him from prison. Portrayed as a feeble old man, which was far from the truth, he escaped with a ten-pound fine and the confiscation of his equipment.

Anyone wishing to blaze a whisky trail through Speyside could find no more fitting starting point than the little glen through which the Livet river runs on its way to join the Spey. It was here in 1824 that George Smith, a successful farmer and distiller, deciding that there was no future in fighting the law, took out a licence and built a new distillery to replace his bothy. The wisdom of his decision was endorsed by a doggerel verse which became popular before very long:

Glenlivet it has castles three,
Drummin, Blairfindy and Deskie,
And also one distillery,
More famous than the castles three.

The region around the Livet had been a popular place to distill whisky for hundreds of years before the first legal distillery was built there in 1824, when George Smith traded in his bothy and founded Glenlivet Distillery (above). He introduced innovations in distilling that produced a whisky considered at that time to be the best in Scotland. Other distillers adopted his improvements, sometimes even the name, but Glenlivet Distillery eventually won exclusive right to the name. It still makes one of the best and most famous malts in the world.

The sentiment behind the verse is still valid, for the three castles are no more than ruins now, but The Glenlivet Distillery continues to enjoy its fame.

In a region where illicit distilling and smuggling had thrived for a hundred years, George Smith's action was considered an arrant piece of treachery. Smugglers who had been his friends and confederates threatened to burn the new distillery down. The convoys of pack horses which he used to take his whisky over mountain tracks to Perth and Edinburgh were ambushed. He was harassed, abused, and reviled. A robust and independent character who did not give way to intimidation, Smith mounted a guard in the distillery every night for years. For his personal defence, he carried with him a pair of pistols given to him by the laird of Aberlour, which can still be seen on show at the distillery today.

George Smith also pioneered improvements in distilling which led to a better and more consistent whisky, and by the time of his death in 1871, Glenlivet Whisky was widely accepted as preeminent among the malt whiskies of Scotland. Other distilleries in the valley of the Spey, although not in the glen of Livet, began to use the name in order to exploit George's success, until a court case etablished that only Glenlivet Distillery was entitled to label its whisky with the name "Glenlivet" alone, although others were allowed to tack the name on after their own. At one time many Speyside distilleries did so, but most of them have abandoned the practice and now rely on their own reputations to sell their whisky.

The Glenlivet continues to be one of the very great whiskies, and in some ways it has become a kind of benchmark for Speyside malts. If any distiller can produce a whisky which will stand comparison with The Glenlivet, he can be well satisfied and not concern himself with trying to surpass it. The merits of a whisky cannot be defined or categorized and will always remain subjective, to be assessed only by the personal taste of the drinker.

The village of Glenlivet was once a thriving village of over forty inhabitants. Today it is home to only two, the postmaster and his wife. Tom Stuart, (opposite) has been the postmaster and the keeper of the lore of Glenlivet for forty years.

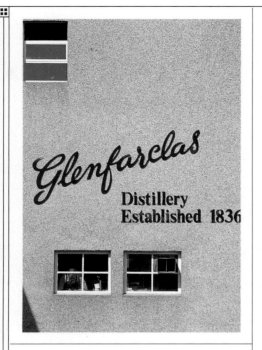

With the help of modern technology, the stillman at Glenfarclas Distillery (opposite) monitors the alcohol in the spirit safe. As soon as any spirit is produced, it is required by the Excise to be kept under lock and key. As the spirit flows from the pot still, it passes through the spirit safe where the stillman watches it flow and decides if it is of the right quality to be collected and sent to the spirit still. From the spirit still, the whisky is put into barrels to age.

❖

Following pages: The stately Rothes Glen Hotel in the town of Rothes is just down the road from Glen Grant Distillery.

George Grant, owner of Glenfarclas, samples a variety of whiskies in the distillery's reception room.

No one should ever be foolhardy enough to single out any one of, say, the twelve or fifteen of the greatest single malts as the best, or even as better than the others.

Having said that, most whisky men would agree that Speyside malts have a flavour and quality that set them apart. They are more full-bodied than malt whiskies from other regions, but for me their supreme merit is that although rich in flavour, they are a "clean" drink, without the medicinal pungency of island whiskies or the slightly oily after-taste in many malts from other parts of Scotland.

Why this should be so is another of the questions about Scotch which has never been satisfactorily answered and probably never will be. Obviously the quality of the water is one reason that so many distilleries have been built near the Spey; the mild, equable climate of the region is another, for distilling good whisky is difficult in extremes of temperature. The local barley is probably not a factor, for although it is used at some distilleries, there is not enough to meet the world's growing demand for Scotch, and much barley is brought up from the Lowlands and from England.

At Glenfarclas Distillery, only a short way along our whisky trail from Glenlivet, I met a man who could speak with authority on barley. Most of the distilleries in Scotland are now owned by the large blending companies, but Glenfarclas is a family business. John Grant, one of the bedraggled "clansmen" from Culloden whom I met in Tulchan Lodge, runs the distillery, and it was at his house which stands beside it that I met Iain McCulloch, a farmer from Easter Ross.

John and Iain had long been adversaries on the curling rink. Curling is a game played on ice by teams of four, in which heavy discs of stone are propelled so that they slide up from one end of a sheet of ice to a target marked at the other end. The object is to stop the "stone" as near to the centre of the target as possible. By twisting the handle of the stone, one can impart spin and curl it round any stones which my be lying in its path. Once an unpretentious game played by farmers and distillers in the Highlands, curling is now an international and highly professional sport, especially in Canada. Scots visiting Canada for the first time are amazed, as I was, by the size and splendid facilities of curling clubs there.

John and his father George, who had retired from the business not long previously, are curling fanatics who will travel almost anywhere for a *bonspiel*, to Switzerland, Sweden, Canada, and the States. They have constructed a small outdoor curling rink behind the distillery, floodlit so that they and their workers can play in winter, when it is dark long before work finishes for the day.

That day we were having a dram of twelve-year-old Glenfarclas to celebrate Iain's success in winning a prize which is presented each year to the farmer growing the best malting barley. Barley used for distilling whisky has to measure up to exacting specifications. It must be low in moisture to avoid the necessity for drying it and low in nitrogen, which is difficult for farmers who must use nitrogen fertilizers. Grain size, straw strength, and enzyme activity are also important if the barley is to give the highest yield. Research funded by the distilling and brewing industries is carried out to develop new and better strains of barley, with prizes awarded yearly to farmers in Scotland

and the rest of Britain as part of a campaign to encourage the growth of varieties which give the best results. Farmers must be romantic fellows at heart because they choose exotic names for prize-winning strains of barley: Natasha, Pipkin, and Halcyon. Not long ago one new strain was christened "Fergie" in honour of the Duchess of York. Some time later a report of the Institute of Brewing made the comment that "Fergie's yield was disappointing", which can only have been unintended humour, as at about that time Fergie gave birth to a bonnie girl.

When we had finished our dram, John Grant took Iain and me round his distillery. We spent most of the time in the still house with its six

copper stills. Distilling whisky is an uncomplicated process, based on the fact that the boiling point of alcohol is lower than that of water. So when the fermented liquid from the washbacks is heated in a still, the alcohol rises as vapour up the neck of the still and is condensed into spirit, while the remaining liquid can be drawn off after the distilling is finished.

Malt whisky is distilled twice, first in a "wash still" and then in a smaller "spirit still". It is in the second distillation that the judgement of the stillman who supervises the process is crucial. The first runnings of spirit coming from the condenser, which are known as "foreshots", are not of the right quality to become whisky, nor are the final runnings, which are known are "feints". It is only the middle cut which is collected and poured into casks to mature.

The stillman must decide when to start collecting this middle cut and when to stop. A greedy distiller, in order to extract the maximum amount of spirit, might allow the collection to continue for a little too long and so spoil the final flavour of his whisky. One sometimes hears blenders in the industry criticizing a malt whisky for being too "feinty".

Besides being whisky country, Speyside is the country of the Clan Grant. From the earliest times the Scots were divided into clans, the members of the clan all having the same ancestry. Until the Battle of Culloden the clans lived as they pleased, feuding and fighting each other as well as the English. Each clan had, and still has, its own

distinctive tartan kilt or plaid: after Culloden, however, the wearing of the kilt was prohibited as part of a drive to subjugate the Highlands. As roads were built up into the north, the power of the clans was broken by English armies.

One finds Grants everywhere on Speyside, engaged in all professions and trades but particularly in distilling. Not far along our whisky trail in the village of Rothes is another distillery which was founded by Grants. Two brothers, James and John, built their Glen Grant Distillery in 1840. The whisky distilled in Glen Grant has a pale, almost lemon colour and a delicate flavour and aroma, and for some reason a particular appeal to Italians. Its success in Italy, where it outsells many of the leading brands of blended Scotch, has been astonishing. At one time people used to say that it was easier to buy a bottle of Glen Grant single malt in Rome than in London.

Major James Grant, son of one of the founders, took over running the distillery in 1872 and was largely responsible for its improvements and expansion. He used to take visitors up the hill on which the distillery stands, through orchards which he had planted, to a bridge over the burn which runs down through the distillery and from which it draws its water. There he had a surprise for them, a glass of Glen Grant from a safe which

he had built into a rock by the burn. Visit the distillery today and you may well be offered the same courteous hospitality.

Rather more than twenty years ago, the company rebuilt an old distillery which stands at the bottom of the hill, not much more than two hundred yards from Glen Grant. Wisely they did not treat it as an extension of Glen Grant, but called it Caperdonich. As it turned out, even though the new distillery used water from the same burn, its whisky is different; similar to Glen Grant but still different. "Kissing cousins", they call the two.

If from Dorothy Brandie's inn one follows the Fiddich upstream, one arrives in Dufftown. To call it a town is a compliment, for only some fifteen hundred people live there, but perhaps the compliment is deserved, as Dufftown has a special importance for all those who admire malt whisky. In the town itself are seven distilleries with an eighth just outside. One-third of the townsfolk depend directly on distilling for their livelihood, while probably another third would not be living and working in Dufftown were there no distilleries there.

Yet another Grant built a distillery more than a hundred years ago, and it was in Dufftown. William Grant was the son of a tailor who had fought with the Gordon Highlanders in the Battle of Waterloo. Ambitious to be his own master, in 1886 William began building a distillery which he named after the valley in which it stands, Glenfiddich. The company of William Grant and Sons is still a family business, but greatly expanded. They own two other malt whisky distilleries, a grain whisky distillery, and a bottling hall in Paisley near Glasgow. It is here that their well-known whisky, called Grants, is blended and bottled.

Sandy Grant Gordon, the third of the clansmen whom I met at Tulchan Lodge, is the company chairman. He is the fourth generation of Grants to work in the business, and the fifth generation has arrived as well, for his son and daughter and his brother Charles's two sons joined not long ago.

Sandy's appearance is deceptive. Though slight and slim and bespectacled, he is immensely strong. Michael Thomson, leader of the expedition that followed Bonnie Prince Charlie's flight to exile,

Dufftown (previous page) is nick-named "the town of seven stills" for its seven distilleries, which provide employ-ment for over a third of the town's residents. With so many distilleries in the same area, one might expect that the whiskies would taste the same, but this is by no means the case. Glenfiddich and Balvenie are owned by the same company and use the same water, yet the two whiskies taste nothing alike.

❖

Following pages: The Spey (overleaf) runs through the heart of the Scottish whisky country.

Strathisla (page 92), the oldest operating distillery in Scotland, has been beautifully restored by its owners, Chivas Brothers, who have made a point of retaining its traditional processes and appearance.

told me that Sandy out-marched them all, never flagging and carrying the heaviest loads. When he was past fifty he took up rock climbing and tackled a difficult climb in winter with the greatest nonchalance.

Not that Sandy is unique. Maybe it is the climate but more likely the whisky, but whatever the reason they breed them strong and hardy in Dufftown. A favourite story at Glenfiddich is of the wedding of Sandy's grandfather. After the wedding, the family, their friends, and no doubt a goodly number of Dufftown folk gathered for a huge *ceilidh* at the distillery. A *ceilidh* is a Highland party, self-generating for the guests provide the entertainment, singing Gaelic songs, piping, and performing Highland dances. The whole of the upper floor of the malt barn had been cleared for the *ceilidh,* which continued well into the night.

Like most malting barns at that time, it had large, shuttered windows which could be kept closed or opened to regulate the temperature inside when barley was spread over the floor to germinate. Because the evening of the wedding was warm, the windows were left open. Sandy's grandfather, wishing to go outside—history does not record why—but forgetting they were on the upper floor of the barn, stepped through one of the openings and tumbled to the ground. His fall would have been all of ten feet, but he got up unhurt, shook his head and exclaimed to those around him, "That was a hell of a long step!"

As well as being hardy, the Grant family are traditionalists. Although today more and more malt whisky distilleries are being equipped as Glenmorangie is, with washbacks made of stainless steel, at Glenfiddich the washbacks are still made of wood. "There is a biological relationship between the wood and the liquid that is fermenting," Sandy says, "which is why we use wood."

Similarly the Grants have resisted the move towards fitting larger pot stills to increase production. The stills at Glenfiddich are of exactly the same size and shape as the original stills installed by

William Grant more than one hundred years ago. They are still heated by coal.

Originally all pot stills were heated by coal, but some years ago a very large proportion of malt whisky distilleries switched to steam heating. Steam is cleaner, and those who believe in it claim that it gives a more even heat and more accurate temperature control. Recently some distilleries have reverted to coal because they feel, as Sandy does, that using steam changes the flavour and character of the whisky. That explanation is an over-simplification, and the arguments on both sides are more complicated and technical, but one thing is certain. The debate, like all debates on the subtler points of distilling, will continue.

Just down the road from Glenfiddich, Sandy's company has another distillery in Dufftown, Balvenie, much smaller than Glenfiddich and arguably even more traditional, with its own floor maltings. Both distilleries draw their water from the Robbie Dubh spring, and so convinced are the Grants that this is the best water in the Highlands for making whisky that they bought one thousand acres of the hillside around it to protect their source.

What, you may well ask, do such traditional methods mean to the flavour of the malt whiskies made by the Grants? Old men with long memories say that the malt whiskies made before the last war were stronger and richer in flavour than the malt whiskies of today, and that, partly because of the new methods that are now used in distilling and partly by design to meet the changing tastes of whisky drinkers, distilleries are now making whiskies with a much lighter, less robust flavour. If this were true, one would expect both Glenfiddich and Balvenie malts to have the strong Celtic character of the past and to make a fierce impact on the palate. Yet to my mind the reverse is true. Both whiskies, and Glenfiddich in particular, are mild and smooth, ideal whiskies to introduce a newcomer to a Scotch malt. That may well be the reason for the success of Glenfiddich, which claims to be the most widely drunk of all single malt Scotch whiskies. Personally I have always had a preference, though only a marginal preference, for Balvenie, which is unfortunate, because only a relatively small quantity of this fine whisky is made each year and it can be as difficult to find as gold dust.

To enjoy and become a connoisseur of Scotch malt whisky it is not necessary to study the science of distilling. However those who do wish to satisfy their inquisitive instincts should retrace their steps along our whisky trail to the Fiddichside Inn, pass it if they have the strength of will to resist dropping in for a dram and a chat with Dorothy, and turn off toward the town of Keith and the Technical Centre attached to Strathisla Distillery. There I found Dr. Dennis Watson.

Strathisla is in any case well worth a visit, for it can claim to be the oldest distillery operating in Scotland, as a Mr. George Taylor began distilling legally at his distillery, which was called Milton at the time, in 1786. It is also one of the most picturesque, with its old waterwheel standing in front

of the carefully restored facade of the distillery buildings. In this attractive but unusual setting, one will find one of the small number of modern, scientific laboratories in the Scotch whisky industry.

Dennis Watson, who obtained his doctorate in applied micro-biology, runs the Technical Centre for Chivas Brothers Limited. Using an impressive battery of scientific instruments and computers, he and his staff carry out the day-to-day tests and analyses which his company believe are needed even in a traditional industry to control production and ensure the highest standards of consistent quality. At the same time they do fundamental research into every facet of the distilling and maturation of whisky.

For me the most intriguing research which they and the other laboratories in the whisky industry are carrying out involves the nature of Scotch itself. Using gas chromatography and other modern techniques of analysis, they have found that there are more than three hundred congenerics or constituents in Scotch, and there are almost certainly many others which have not yet been identified. What scientists are trying to do is to relate the composition of any particular whisky to its aroma and, ultimately, to its flavour. Volunteers are recruited to "nose" a selection of whisky samples in the way that blenders do and then describe them using a number of standard descriptive terms.

This part of the process cannot be done with scientific instruments because, as Dennis Watson

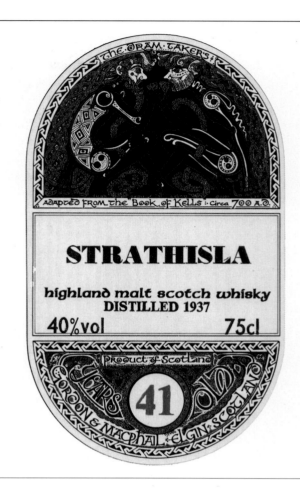

says, there is no substitute for the human nose. The same is true, of course, for the human palate. Taste is purely subjective. If you and I taste the same whisky, we have no means of knowing whether the actual flavours which our separate senses of taste record are identical. Surely this must mean that research into flavour can never produce any finite answers. Scientists will never be able to say that if one could produce whiskies at separate distilleries with exactly the same proportions of the three hundred-odd congenerics, they would also taste the same.

All research can do is to provide some very good guidelines to help the distiller. Brilliant scientist and delightful fellow though he is, Dennis

Watson will never be able to lay down a formula and set of standard instructions which, if the distiller followed them, would produce a uniform, homogeneous, identically-flavoured Scotch whisky. I find this reassuring. Even so, one must not in any way belittle the work that science and research are doing to maintain and improve the quality and consistency of the whisky made in Scotland.

The malt whisky made at Strathisla is rare because, as they will tell you at the distillery, most of what they make becomes the heart of one of the best known of all blended whiskies, Chivas Regal. Some malt whisky experts hold the view that Strathisla is a woman's whisky. They do not mean that disparagingly. Today more and more women appreciate Scotch, and very often, when they choose a single malt, they are looking more for delicate subtlety than for bravura. And this they will certainly find in Strathisla.

There are distilleries on both sides of the River Spey, some with names derived from Gaelic, the meanings of which have often been lost because of changes in spelling. Right on the north bank of the river and with glorious views down its valley are Tamdhu and Knockando. For those who work in the distilleries the temptation on warm summer days to slip down to the water and make a cast or two with the salmon rod must be overwhelming; judging by the magnificent salmon which hangs in a glass case on the walls of the manager's office in Tamdhu, temptation is not always resisted. The malt whiskies made at both distilleries are mainly used in the blends marketed by the companies which own them—Tamdhu in The Famous Grouse and Knockando in J and B Rare—though each is also increasingly available as a single malt. Perhaps because the two distilleries are not very far apart, I always feel I can detect two characteristics which they share; lightness and elegance. Otherwise I find them very different, with Tamdhu inclined to sweetness, while Knockando has a kind of fragrance which is very distinctive.

A short distance up the hill that lies behind them is Cardhu. On my last visit there I was delighted to find that Evan Cattanach, whom I had known on Islay, was now the manager. I first met Evan in Bessie Campbell's house above Laphroaig, and now, by coincidence, he was working in a distillery which had also been owned and run by a woman, although more than a hundred years previously.

Before 1823 Cardow farm—pronounced "cardoo"—like scores of others in the Highlands, had a distillery which it operated surreptitiously, smuggling the whisky to nearby towns of Elgin and Forres, where there were always plenty of people anxious to buy it. In 1824 John Cumming, the tenant-farmer, took out a licence under the new Act of Parliament and ran both the farm and the distillery until his death in 1839, whereupon they passed to his son Lewis. Thirty years later Lewis died, leaving a widow, Elizabeth, and three young children. A woman of great energy and resourcefulness, Elizabeth continued to farm and to run the distillery, so successfully in fact, that

At the beautiful and remote Cardhu Distillery (right), a worker stencils the year and the quantity of whisky each cask contains on newly-filled barrels (below). Evan Cattanach (opposite page), manager of Cardhu, displays a belly flask.

❖

Following pages: Allan Shiach, the chairman of Macallan Distillery, poses on one of the sherry casks for which his distillery is famous (page 101). Macallan is one of only a few distilleries which routinely markets single malts at different ages; Macallan's twelve-year-old and eighteen-year-old malts are both readily available in the U.K. and the U.S.A. Before taking over Macallan, Allan Shiach lived in Hollywood where, under the pen name Allan Scott, he wrote the screenplays for such films as "Don't Look Back" starring Julie Christie and Donald Sutherland, and "The Awakening" with Charlton Heston.

she was able to build a completely new one and used the name "Cardhu" as a trademark for her whisky. In 1893 she sold the distillery to John Walker and Sons of Kilmarnock, a firm which was to achieve world renown later with its Johnnie Walker Black Label and Red Label blended whiskies.

The malt whisky which Evan Cattanach now makes is a classic Speyside malt, clean and uncomplicated in its aroma and leaving a satisfying richness lingering on the palate long after the last sip. About thirty years ago Cardhu, as the distillery is now named, was extended and enlarged, and has become one of the most elegant and spacious of the malt whisky distilleries, without losing its traditional character.

It also stands alone in remote, unspoilt country, with the cottages of those who work there clustered around it and a church and school immediately behind. Visit it and you will sense the timelessness of whisky and the tranquility of those who spend their lives distilling it. You will find few men by the mash tun or the washbacks or in the still house, and those you do see will move in a leisurely way, closing a valve or checking an instrument or peering into the bubbles of fermenting liquid without fuss, as though they know that they cannot hasten the unhurried pace of nature. And in the warehouses the casks sleep, row upon row, stretching back into the darkness, waiting years until the mysterious alchemy which transforms an untamed spirit into a smooth, mellow whisky has finished its work and they can be rolled out into the sunshine.

Maturation is the final stage in the making of whisky and, since all trails must end, we can do no better than end ours a few miles to the north of Cardhu at Macallan Distillery. Maturation plays an important part in determining the character and quality of a whisky, and at Macallan they are convinced that they have discovered the style of maturation which produces the finest single malt whisky. In one respect it is unique.

All Scotch whisky must age for at least three years in casks made from oak. That bare statement may give the impression that maturation is a straightforward business, not likely to require a great deal of skill and judgement, nor to provoke passionate differences of opinion. In reality the distiller—and the blender—has many options each of which will fundamentally affect the character of the whisky when it is drawn from its cask. The size and type of cask used, the kind of warehouse in which it is kept, and the length of time for which it is allowed to mature are just three of those options.

The basic principle of maturation is that since the oak from which the casks are made is permeable, air can reach the spirit inside and by a process of oxidization remove its more fiery constituents, leaving, after a space of years, a smooth, mellow whisky. Like so much that is said about Scotch, that is an oversimplification, a kind of idiot's guide, but even scientists cannot tell us much more. Scholarly treatises have been written on the chemistry of maturation, but in truth most of them have been little more than scientific speculation. .

We do not fully understand the reasons for the remarkable changes that take place in the character of whisky as it lies maturing. And so the distiller must rely on his judgement, and his judgement is based on experience. Those who run Macallan Distillery know that in the past when their whisky has been filled into a particular kind of cask and allowed to lie in a warehouse at a certain temperature and humidity and then taken out after a given number of years, it had a certain character and flavour. They know that if they repeat the process, they will have a whisky which, apart from infinitesimally small differences that even a trained nose will be hard pressed to detect, will be the same.

The wood most commonly used for casks in which Scotch is matured is either Spanish oak or American oak. Oak from other countries, France for example, has proved to be unsuitable. For many years Scotch was matured almost solely in casks of Spanish oak, which had previously held sherry. The British have always drunk large quantities of sherry, which was shipped from Spain in oak casks. Once emptied of sherry, these casks proved excellent for maturing Scotch whisky. In more recent times the world demand for Scotch increased so rapidly that there were no longer enough sherry casks available. Distillers, canny Scots as they are and knowing the cost of having oak imported and made into casks, looked around for another source of ready-made ones, and they found it in the United States.

Regulations for making Bourbon whiskey stipulate that a cask may only be used once. When I asked the reason for this stipulation, which the distillers of Bourbon have tried without success to have changed, I was told gruffly: "Because in the States the timber lobby is more powerful than the whiskey lobby." Whatever the reason, each year hundreds of thousands of American casks are now broken down into staves, shipped across the Atlantic, reassembled, and filled with new Scotch whisky.

Yet another cause of controversy in the making of Scotch is what effect the type of cask used for maturation has on the flavour of the whisky. A chemical reaction between the wood and the new spirit is the basic reason for the change in the character of whisky as it matures, but the kind of cask into which it is poured also has an influence. Malt whisky matured in a sherry cask is more golden in colour than whisky kept in an American whiskey cask, and most people would agree that it is also a little sweeter. The blenders who are responsible for producing the brands of blended Scotch which dominate the world's markets today take a proportion of whisky matured in sherry casks and usually mix it with a larger proportion of whisky from American oak casks, thus striking a balance in the blend which appeals to a wider range of tastes.

At Macallan they hold a more sophisticated—and more dogmatic—view of how their whisky should be matured. Sherry itself comes in a wide variety of styles and flavours according to the type of grape from which it is made, ranging from the very light, dry Fino to the sweet, golden Oloroso. The directors of Macallan Distillery are convinced that to achieve the finest flavour and bouquet, their whisky should be matured only in casks which measure up to their exacting requirements, and each year they travel to the *bodegas* of Jerez to select the casks which they wish to buy.

Their dedication has certainly been rewarded, for Macallan whisky, whether it is bottled at twelve, fifteen or eighteen years, is a very fine single malt. Some writers have described it as "fruity", but I find that not an apt description. It may be fanciful, but for me all of the Highland Malt whiskies have a flavour reminiscent of the country in which they were made, the richness of the peat and heather, the broom which fills the landscape with great clusters of brilliant yellow, the poppies which stand among the corn, and the wild flowers along the roadside. It is this flavour, impossible to describe with any single adjective, which finds its most eloquent expression in the whisky made at Macallan. For many years it was not easily available outside of Scotland, but this is changing now and changing rapidly, largely because of one man.

Over the centuries the Scots have created an image for themselves as proud and independent, slow to accept change, and, on first acquaintance at least, reserved and even a little dour. Anyone who goes to Macallan Distillery expecting to find the chairman of the company in this traditional mould will be in for a surprise. Allan Shiach is far removed from most people's idea of a whisky distiller. His family have been a part of Macallan ever since his great-grandfather acquired the distillery, but Allan first made his career in entertainment, and in the United States. Artistic, extrovert and witty, he was once a presenter on television and is one of the most talented and successful scriptwriters in the film business. His younger brother Peter ran Macallan Distillery until his death of cancer at a tragically early age, after which Allan returned from the States to become the chairman.

In a short space of time his vitality and his ideas made a great impact. Macallan single malt remains the same, and in truth there was little to improve in its character or in the way it was being distilled and matured, but its marketing and promotion are now very much in Allan's style, original and bold. Advertisements for Macallan, unlike those of other internationally marketed drinks, are not plastered across the billboards alongside freeways nor on full pages of glossy magazines. Instead they are so small that they may be unnoticed, off-beat in a tongue-in-cheek style, not so much selling Macallan to the reader as trying to make him believe he has discovered it for himself.

The concept behind such advertising may be more subtle than it appears. People who know their whiskies may write and talk about the different malt whiskies to be found in Scotland. They may rhapsodize over the flavour of a particular single malt. They may even be bold enough, as several distinguished authors have been, to make a list of what they believe to be the dozen finest malts. What they are doing is no more than putting up signposts, for the real fascination of Scotch whisky lies in discovery, in finding out for oneself the pleasure which each of the whiskies from the 103 malt distilleries of Scotland can offer.

The Blender's Art

Remote and aloof in the forest, Blair Castle in Perthshire, with its dazzlingly white walls and turrets, might easily be the setting for a children's fairy tale. Looking up at its towers one almost expects to see a princess leaning out of a window to let down her golden hair to a waiting prince below. Perthshire is the county where the Highlands of Scotland really begin. Travelling north, as soon as one crosses the River Tay, the landscape changes, pasture land giving way to splendid forests of pine, fir, and spruce, which in their turn give way to great rolling moors and gaunt mountains. On the soft day I arrived, the castle was the setting for the Atholl Gathering and Highland Games.

Soon the meadow in the castle grounds, around which more than three thousand folk had gathered, would be a crowded arena. Kilted giants would stagger under the weight of a seventeen-foot tree trunk, holding it upright before tossing it to flop over lengthwise on the ground. Wee girls would dance the Highland Fling. Pipers in the full splendour of Highland dress would vie with each other in playing the *strathspeys* and marches of the *ceol beg*, or "little music", and the elaborate laments of the *piobaireachd*, the classic form of bagpipe music.

As we waited expectantly for the arrival of the chieftain of the games, little was happening. In a far corner athletes were limbering and dancers

In the hills of Perthshire stands Blair Castle (above), the ancestral home of His Grace the Duke of Atholl (opposite). Behind him on the castle wall hangs the portrait of his ancestor, the first Duke. Head of the Clan Murray, the Duke of Atholl is the only private citizen who is allowed to have his own army; today the Atholl Highlanders are only a ceremonial fighting force, but it is still considered a great distinction to be asked to join.

Each year the Duke hosts the Atholl Gathering and Highland Games in the castle meadow, where over three thousand Scots gather for an afternoon of athletic competition, music, dancing, and, of course, whisky.

❖

Following pages: Deerstalkers search for stags (page 108). Whisky blender Donald Mackinlay (page 109) stalks deer on Loch Con.

were rehearsing their steps soundlessly while kilted officials walked importantly back and forward across the meadow, holding programmes and judging sheets.

At last the chieftain arrived and was piped to his place by the Atholl Pipers. His Grace the Duke of Atholl, head of the Clan Murray, has a distinction which no one in Britain shares: he is the only private citizen allowed to have his own army. The Atholl Highlanders parade regularly, and any Scot would be proud to be invited to join them. That day they were at the Highland Games, parading with their own pipe band.

Blair Castle, which sheltered Prince Charles Edward on his glorious march to England in 1745 and again on his inglorious retreat, is not really in whisky country. Perthshire has only a handful of distilleries; Aberfeldy and Blair Athol near Pitlochry, Dalwhinnie to the north, and Edradour, the smallest distillery in Scotland. Edradour, which lies on the estate of the Duke of Atholl only a few miles from his castle, is run by just three men. It is an exquisite distillery in miniature, where a visitor can watch and almost share in the process of whisky-making and have his dram, all in the space of a few square feet and in a few minutes if he so

wishes, although it would be a crime to hurry over the dram.

So when Donald Mackinlay came to the games that day, it was not on whisky business. Donald, whom I first met some years before on the island of Jura, is a whisky blender, but he is a sportsman too. He has an estate in Trinafour, a short distance away from Blair Castle, where he shoots his own grouse moor and fishes his own loch.

On the morning following our meeting at the games, I drove over to his house, and the door was opened to my knock by his youngest daughter Mary, known to everyone, for reasons which no one can remember, as Muff.

"Daddy's up on the hill looking at the water," Muff told me.

On Jura, Donald and I had talked of water and its importance to the distiller. Did this mean, I wondered, that he was now broadening his interests in Scotch and distilling his own, secretly on the hill behind his house? Muff put on her Wellingtons and led me up through the copse at the back of the house. We found her father anxiously examining the course of a small burn that ran down the hill. No, he assured me, he was not about to branch out into moonshining. The spring which fed the burn was the source of the water supply of his house, and the burn was not running as it should. We went down to the house and agreed that because it was such a beautiful day, we would take a picnic lunch out to the loch.

Muff volunteered to cut the sandwiches, and while she was working in the kitchen, Donald and I talked about his work as a whisky blender. Blended Scotch whisky is by definition a blend of Scotch malt whiskies and Scotch grain whiskies. Malt whisky is made only from malted barley in the traditional copper pot stills in which the Scots have made whisky for centuries. Grain whisky is made from a mixture of malted barley, unmalted barley, and other cereals, most often maize, in the patent still which came into use in the 1830s. Distillation in the patent still is a continuous process, and it produces a whisky of a higher strength, and consequently less flavour and character, than pot still whisky. It is perfectly possible to continue distillation in a patent still to a point when all the flavour of the distillate is removed, and one then has "neutral" or flavourless alcohol. Grain whisky made in Scotland, however, must by law be taken from the still when it still retains the flavour derived from the cereals used in its distillation. It must also be properly matured in exactly the same way as malt whisky, in casks made from oak. In some other countries a blended whiskey may be made up of a mixture of whisky and neutral spirit. This is not allowed in Scotland, and the difference is important.

Any of the well-known blended Scotches will contain between fifteen and fifty different single whiskies—Highland Malts, Lowland Malts, and Islays—as well as grain whiskies, blended in proportions laid down in a formula developed over the years by the blender. Once the formula has been established, it is the responsibility of the blender and his staff to make sure that it is maintained. Their objective is to produce a Scotch with its own distinctive flavour and one that will remain consistent year after year, no matter what variations there may be in the constituent whiskies.

From a cupboard in his study, Donald took some samples of different single whiskies for me to "nose". Whisky blenders work entirely by their sense of smell and have an extraordinary ability to identify not only the regions from which a whisky comes and the distillery in which it has been made, but also its age and the type of cask in which it has been matured.

The whiskies Donald gave me to nose that morning were Longmorn, a Highland Malt from Speyside, Lagavulin from Islay, Glenkinchie from the Lowlands, and Cameronbrig, a grain whisky that is marketed as a single whisky. He also poured me two samples of Balmenach, another Speyside malt, one of which had been matured in sherry wood and the other in an American barrel. I found I could detect the differences between the samples fairly easily and began to wonder whether I might not have missed my true vocation in life. Blenders occupy a key position in a whisky company and are handsomely rewarded.

Next I was given three samples of the same single malt from Convalmore, a distillery in Dufftown. All had been matured in sherry casks, but for different lengths of time—six, ten, and twelve years. This time I found the differences in the samples much more difficult to detect. When I suggested that this might be because my nose was

growing tired, its perceptiveness dulled by the repeated sniffing of strong spirit, Donald smiled.

"In the sample room of my company," he said, "I may have to nose more than a hundred samples before lunch."

When Muff joined us with the packed picnic basket, we climbed into an elderly Land Rover, took aboard an even more elderly Labrador, and set out for Loch Con. The Labrador's name, Muff told me, was Breac, which in Gaelic means "spotted". He had been born with a white spot on one of his paws which had since vanished, but the name had stuck.

The winding, bumpy track to Donald's loch wound up on the moors, with heather stretching into the distance on both sides. In places the heather was black and charred where it had been burnt neatly in long strips some fifteen to twenty yards wide. Donald explained that his family had gone out and burnt the heather, which had to be done to promote new growth, for it was on the new shoots that young grouse fed.

The grouse shooting season starts on "The Glorious Twelfth" of August each year, and the first birds shot are flown to London for gourmets in fashionable clubs and restaurants to eat the same day. Grouse shooting has such a cachet now that visitors from abroad are happy to pay huge sums for the privilege of one day on the Scottish moors.

When we reached his loch, Donald and I sat in the sun drinking malt whisky which he had brought with him in a beautiful old silver flask, while Muff threw sticks into the water which

Breac, in spite of his age, plunged in to retrieve like an excited puppy. The day was unbelievably clear, with no hint of haziness, and the loch was a deep, almost indigo, blue. Beyond it heather moors stretched to the west, unbroken and endless, it seemed. At another time and in different weather the loneliness and the overwhelming emptiness might have been frightening, but in the sunshine and with the reassurance of familiar sounds—the lapping of water against the bank, the happy barking of a dog, a young girl's laughter—it was a day for tranquillity and idleness, conversation between friends, and the shared, unhurried pleasure of a fine whisky.

Our conversation was about whisky. What else? Donald told me that to ensure that a blended whisky remained consistent in quality and flavour, the blender might from time to time have to make adjustments to the formula. If, for example, a particular single whisky was not up to standard or, for some reason, the company found itself short of it, the blender would have to compensate by using more of a different but similar whisky. A sample was always drawn from every cask which was to be used in the blend, and the blender and his assistants would have to nose it and decide whether it was fully matured and not tainted or spoiled in any way.

From time to time the notion is put forth by some people in the business that the legal definition of Scotch, and in particular of blended Scotch, should be made more rigorous. One suggestion was that a blend should have to contain a minimum and a maximum proportion of malt and grain whiskies. Another was that the constituent whiskies should all be listed on the label. Donald was not in favour of the idea.

"It would give no guarantee of quality," he said.

The inclusion of any particular single whisky in a blend, in whatever proportions, is no guide to its quality. A blend made up of only single whiskies selected from those that are recognized as being the finest in Scotland would not necessarily be a good blend; indeed, as some whiskies are incompatible with others, it might to all intents and purposes be undrinkable.

"Blending is largely a matter of striking a balance," Donald explained. "If, for example, I were to make a blend with a large proportion of island whiskies, I would need to balance them with the lighter, less full-flavoured Lowland Malts."

We had finished our sandwiches and were lingering over our dram when we spotted a herd of red deer on a distant hill. Deer stalking is also a popular sport in Scotland, but it is not merely sport for sport's sake. In Perthshire, as on Jura and in other parts of the Highlands, the number of deer allowed to roam and graze on the hills must be controlled. The land can only support a limited number, and if the herds grew too numerous, the

deer would starve to death. The law of nature no longer controls the size of the population, for the wild animals which would prey on deer are now all extinct in Scotland. Therefore, every year the landowners in Donald's part of Perthshire meet to decide how many must be culled by shooting.

That afternoon I left Donald at Trinafour, digging out the burn, and drove towards Perth, not along the main road to the south but by Loch Rannoch and Loch Tummel, two names familiar even to those Scots who have never visited Scotland, mentioned as they are in the song that every Scottish bairn learns, "The Road to the Isles". Beyond Rannoch stands the graceful, solitary mountain of Schiehallion. Some say that the Gaelic name means "The Fairy Hill". Others insist that the correct translation is "The Maiden's Breast". The two names, one supposes, need not necessarily contradict each other.

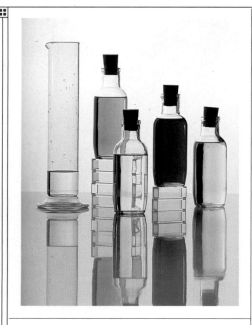

A blender works entirely by his sense of smell. By "nosing" a sample of malt whisky, Robertson & Baxter's managing director Ian Good and John MacPhail, former chairman of the Scotch Whisky Association (opposite), can determine not only the distillery in which it was made, but also its age and the type of cask in which it was matured. The type of cask affects a whisky's colour; the samples (above) are, from left to right: water, twelve-year-old whisky aged in a light sherry cask, new whisky, whisky aged in a dark sherry cask, and whisky aged in an American Bourbon cask.

❖

Following pages: Dr. Alan Brown in the sample room of Robertson & Baxter (page 112).

Blender Alan Reid noses a whisky sample (page 113).

Samples of whiskies are sent to the blenders by distilleries (page 115).

I had been invited to dinner that evening in Perth, and as I drove, it struck me that blending a good Scotch is similar to arranging a dinner party. Whiskies are like people; some have strong flavours and strong characters, others are more delicate and subtle, still others lack personality but are good blending whiskies. No hostess would invite to her dinner party only extroverts, good raconteurs, or people of strong opinions. For the dinner to be a success, she must also invite other guests, pleasant people of equable temperament, good listeners who will bring out the best of the lions. And so it is with blending. If in your blend you have chosen, for example, The Glenlivet, Macallan, Laphroaig, Glen Grant, and Mortlach, you must complement them with several lesser malts in order to have a smooth, harmonious blend.

A few weeks later, on another trip around Scotland, I met another whisky blender. Alan Reid has his magnificent, roomy sample room in the offices of Robertson and Baxter, a Glasgow whisky firm whose history goes back more than a hundred years. That morning Alan showed me some of the hundreds of bottles on shelves around the sample room, each of them holding a sample of a single malt or grain whisky or of a number of singles "vatted" together. The glasses which blenders use to nose whisky are tulip-shaped, narrowing towards the top to allow a maximum concentration of aroma and bouquet. The blender pours a small amount of the whisky he wishes to examine into the glass and then adds an equal amount of plain water. This helps to release the aroma of the whisky, as anyone can discover with a simple experiment. Most sample glasses are made from plain glass, but that morning I noticed a set of blue ones on a shelf. Alan explained that these were used occasionally to compare different samples, when blenders did not want their judgements to be influenced by the colour of the whisky. We began talking about colour.

Like brandy, rum, and all distilled spirits, whisky has no colour when it comes off the still. The new spirit will draw some colour

from the cask as it matures, the depth of colour varying according to the type and age of cask. A sherry cask will impart a golden colour. Scotch matured in a cask that has been used several times over a space of forty to fifty years will be much paler than that from a new cask.

This variation in colour poses a problem for the blender. Since the colour of the different single whiskies he uses in his blend vary, the final blend will also vary from one batch to another; if whisky drinkers were to find that a blend varied in colour from one bottle to another, they might believe that the blend was changing. Small quantities of colour, in the form of caramelized sugar, may

therefore be added to the blend to bring the whisky up to a standard, consistent colour.

Alan Reid had a friend with him in his sample room that day, another Alan. Dr. Alan Brown has worked for many years in the whisky business, mainly in research and development, and is now a consultant. He told me how three or four years previously he had been asked to develop a new blend of Scotch, mainly for sale in France, which was to be called "Grassy Green".

When I asked the reason for what seemed to be an extraordinary name, Alan Brown told me that the whisky had a flavour reminiscent of grass. More than one single malt has this characteristic

and in devising the blend he had chosen only those malts and blended them with grain whisky.

I must have seemed sceptical, for now the two Alans produced a selection of whisky samples for me to nose. The first one they handed me had a faint but very distinctive aroma which seemed familiar, but which I found difficult to identify. After a time I recognized it as the aroma of black-currants. As I nosed the sample again, the aroma seemed to change gradually into one which was entirely different.

Alan was not surprised. Nosing a whisky, he said, was in a way similar to an optical illusion. If you were, for example, to look at a drawing of a cube for long enough, it would appear to change and you would have the impression that you were not looking at a cube but into an empty room. In the same way the aroma one thinks one can identify in a sample of whisky will often change into a completely different aroma.

The main difficulty in talking about the flavour of whisky lies in finding words to describe it. The aroma may be compared with black currants or grass or pear drops, but at best these are only approximations: when one sips the whisky one certainly does not get the flavours normally asso-ciated with black currants or grass or pear drops. Teams of blenders, or "nosing panels", who work regularly together can describe whiskies with expressions like these and each will know what aroma the others are talking about, but the lay-man may well find them as incomprehensible as a foreign language.

We nosed several samples that morning and the two Alans not only agreed on the aromas they were finding but were also able to account for any unusual variations by, for example, changes in the quality of the malt that had been used or slight faults in the processes. Most of what they were saying was too esoteric and scientific for me to understand. After my conversation with Donald Mackinlay a few days previously, I had been pre-sumptuous enough to believe that I understood the art of blending. Now I realized that making whisky was and would always remain for me a vast, unmapped territory with only a few simple sign-posts to follow.

It will be the same for most people, but even amateurs can play the blender. Collect a few bottles of single whiskies, some of the lesser-known but still very fine malts if you can procure them—Clynelish from the far north of Scotland, Glendronach from Aberdeenshire, Tomintoul and Aberlour from Speyside, Springbank, one of the two whiskies made on the Mull of Kintyre, and Rosebank, which many people believe to be the finest of the Lowland Malts. Match them against samples taken from brands of blended Scotches. See if you can detect the presence of the Islay Malt Lagavulin in White Horse whisky, which is owned by the same company. Compare a standard blend like Bell's, for example, with a twelve-year-old like Chivas Regal. You will never become a blender, but the experience will sharpen your sense of both smell and taste and add a new dimension to your appreciation of Scotch whisky.

From Little Aphids

Since the Middle Ages, Scotland and France have always had a special relationship. The Auld Alliance, as it is affectionately called, might have started, as many lasting friendships do, only on the bond of a common hatred and a wish to cause as much inconvenience as possible to the Auld Enemy, England. Over the centuries, however, it grew into a close understanding, with strong and lasting cultural and commercial ties.

The elegance and manners of the Scottish court up to the Reformation owed much to French influence, and a young Scot who wished to complete his education would travel not in England but in France. At a time when communications in Scotland were meagre—there were no roads fit for wheeled traffic north of the River Tay until after the first rebellion in 1715—it was as easy to take a ship from northern ports for France as for England. Until quite modern times, an Act of the Scottish Parliament had granted all Frenchmen dual nationality, Scottish as well as French.

Because of this French connection, the Scots long ago developed a liking for the wines of France, and to satisfy their taste large quantities of the best wines were being imported from Bordeaux and Burgundy by the middle of the nineteenth century. At that time whisky was being drunk almost only in Scotland, and it was Scottish wine merchants rather than distillers who first saw the enormous possibilities of markets outside the country. They began

shipping Scotch first to England and then around the world. In doing so they were helped by one of those unexpected accidents of fate which so often lead to great changes in the fortunes of men. America, quite fortuituosly, played a part in this accident.

Throughout the first half of the nineteenth century, beer and gin were the drinks of English working people, while the leisured classes drank wine and brandy. Wealthy young rakes, after dining at their London clubs, would make for the card tables where they drank brandy and soda, and the same drink would be served in the evenings in the drawing rooms of gentlemen landowners.

Then came a series of minor disasters for the French wine trade. Many vineyards were affected by a form of mildew which resulted in a succession of poor crops. In the hope of correcting this, vine stocks were imported from America on the theory that good new "blood" was needed to restore health. Instead the American vines brought a major disaster—an aphid called phylloxera, a bug related to greenfly. In a very short space of time phylloxera ravaged France's vineyards, destroying over half of them. Wine became scarce and expensive, and so in due course did brandy.

Up until that time Scotch had been sold mainly in casks, and it was customary for restaurants, hotels, and householders to order it in hogsheads. Now, to exploit the new market offered by the demise of brandy and to reach more modest customers, wine merchants in Scotland began blending malt and grain whiskies together and selling the blends in bottles under their own labels. Their reason for blending may have been that they felt the full-bodied flavour of malt whisky would be unacceptable to English palates accustomed to the bland, insipid taste of brandy and soda. Whatever the reason, their decision was justified, for it marked the beginning of an era in which, as an Italian journalist, carried away by the phenomenal success of single malts in Italy, told me with unrestrained hyperbole, "Scotch whisky succeeded where Alexander and Caesar and Napoleon and Hitler failed. It conquered the world."

The invasion of England by Scotch whisky was certainly helped by Queen Victoria, who took a sudden fancy to Scotland, even to the extent of making her children wear the kilt when they were on holiday at Balmoral Castle and making the lugubrious Scot, John Brown, her personal servant. She visited Lochnagar Distillery which stands just outside Balmoral, tasted its whisky, and is said to have approved. Her example was soon followed by scores of wealthy Englishmen who, anxious to please their sovereign, began visiting Scotland, buying sporting estates, and building themselves pretentious mansions in a strikingly hideous, baronial style.

In 1897, hoping to take advantage of this new market, William Gloag, son of the Perth wine merchant Mathew Gloag of Mathew Gloag and Sons, decided to sell his own blended Scotch and chose to call it "The Famous Grouse", a name singularly appropriate for a whisky from Scotland's leading sporting country. It soon became known to Englishmen who came to shoot and stalk and fish in Perthshire, many of whom became loyal customers, ordering it by the case to be sent to their homes in the south and drinking no other brand.

Scotch whisky is the drink of power and prestige in the twentieth century, but its rise to prominence was both recent and unexpected. Brandy, neat and with soda, was the spirit of choice in London society while whisky was still almost unheard of outside of the Scottish Highlands. Then crop failures struck the French vineyards in the late nineteenth century, and as the ensuing brandy shortage worsened, the demand for Scotch soared.

In an attempt to take advantage of this new market, wine merchants such as Matthew Gloag and Sons of Perth, founded by the great-grandfather of Matthew Gloag (page 120), began to make the first blended Scotches, often using specially-designed labels to appeal to customers (page 121). Gloag introduced The Famous Grouse in 1897, aimed at the English gentry who built country estates and hunted deer and grouse on the Scottish moors. Many of these manors, like Tulchan Lodge (below), have since been converted into grand hotels.

Mathew Gloag and Sons were not the only wine merchants in Perth to become involved in the whisky business before the century's end. The firm of John Dewar and Sons had been founded in 1846 and had premises in the High Street. John's two sons, John and Thomas, became partners in the business, with John running the business in Perth while Tom opened an office in London. A flamboyant character, Tom was an outstanding salesman and may well have done more than any other single man to make Scotch whisky known round the world. In 1892 he set out from Liverpool for New York on a sales trip which was to last two years and circle the globe. He visited twenty-six countries and returned having established thirty-two agencies for his brand.

Tom fancied himself an author and described his travels with many amusing anecdotes in a book which he had illustrated with drawings by well-known artists and by himself. One of the best known of his sayings—"Dewarisms" he called them—was: "Do right and fear no man; don't write and fear no woman." Like his great friend King Edward VII, he was fond of fast cars and fast horses, but unlike Edward not of women, fast or slow, and never married. Both he and his brother John were knighted and later made barons, a unique distinction in the whisky business as far as I can tell.

One of the curious aspects of the history of Scotch is that the wine merchants who first pioneered the trade in blended whisky were not based in Scotland's two main cities of Edinburgh and Glasgow. Two already mentioned were based in Perth, while a third, John Walker, came from the small coal-mining town of Kilmarnock. Like most other similar firms they were not wine merchants as we understand the expression today, but licensed grocers, a particularly Scottish form of retail business. For years after its establishment in 1820, the firm remained very much a family concern, with John Walker being succeeded by his son Alexander, whose own two sons joined the business as well. In the years leading up to the 1914 war the firm became the largest blenders and bottlers of Scotch whisky. One prominent factor in its success was certainly the advertisement which the Walkers commissioned in 1908. The poster, with its portrait of a top-hatted dandy and the caption "Johnnie Walker—born 1820, still going strong" has been recognized by advertising professionals as one of the most effective creations of their trade.

As whisky became more widely known and more popular in England and abroad, the business of blending and bottling became extremely competitive. The companies which came to the forefront were those who were most skillful at marketing their brands; they succeeded, in the main, because they found good agents in overseas territories and backed up their endeavours with clever advertising and promotion. But some companies relied, for their initial success at least, on the personal energy and flair of a single individual.

One such firm was James Buchanan and Company. Born in Canada of Scottish parents who later returned to Scotland, Buchanan started his career as an office boy in a shipping company. Not until the age of thirty did he enter the whisky trade, when he began work as an agent in London for Charles Mackinlay and Company. Five years later he started his own company on borrowed capital. A tall man with an aristocratic face and manner—he dressed like an aristocrat, too, always elegant whether in top hat and frock coat or in his dress kilt—Buchanan promoted his whisky with a combination of cheek and flair. He managed to persuade leading restaurants and hotels to stock his blend, which later became known by the colour of its black and white label. His greatest coup was when he obtained a contract for supplying the House of Commons with whisky for its Members Bar, a fact which he exploited to get as much publicity as he could. Many stories are told of his ingenuity in promoting Black and White, but one which caused great amusement concerns his promotion not of his whisky but of himself. The story may well be apocryphal, but it reflects the admiration which his contemporaries felt for his canny Scottish shrewdness.

At that time it was generally believed—and it may well have been true—that knighthoods and peerages could be secured by making a sufficiently impressive contribution to the party funds of whatever government was in power. Lloyd George, the Prime Minister in 1922, was no friend of the drinks industry—he even thought of imposing prohibition in Britain at one time—but he agreed that Buchanan should have a peerage in return for a suitable political donation. Buchanan chose the title of Lord Woolavington and, distrustful of politicians, signed the cheque which he handed

over with that name, thus making certain that it could not be cashed until he had been invested with his title.

During the First World War the Scotch whisky trade was badly hit by Government restrictions and increases in duty. Prohibition, although in the long term it helped to establish the reputation of Scotch in the United States, was another blow, preventing any immediate recovery. In the 1930s sales began to pick up, and the years following the Second World War saw the beginning of a phenomenal expansion which was to make Scotch the most widely drunk spirit in the world.

In order to meet the rapidly growing demand, most of the major whisky companies were forced to invest in new blending and bottling halls. The bottling of whisky is a relatively straight-forward operation, lacking any of the romance and mystery to be found in distilling. After the single whiskies, malt as well as grain, have been passed by the blender, the casks are taken to the blending hall where they are emptied into a trough. From there the whisky is pumped into blending vats where it is thoroughly mixed, or "roused", and colour added if it is required. The newly-blended whisky will then be filled once more into casks in which it will be left to "marry" for a period of between three and twelve months. This honeymoon period allows the different single whiskies to get to know each other and meld into a harmonious blend. Finally, the blend is filled into bottles which are capped, labelled, and packed in cases ready for despatch.

The distilling of whisky has remained a traditional process in which nature and time play a greater part than science; it is in bottling that modern technology has helped to make the greatest advances. Bottling and packing at high speed were essential to produce Scotch in sufficient quantities to meet growing demand, and in the last few decades several large new bottling halls have been built. In the latest and most modern, built near Loch Lomond, almost every stage in the process, from the blending to

The Scottish countryside will always be the home of malt whisky, but today, as the demand for malts and blends continues to grow, the centres of Scotland's billion-dollar whisky trade are the major cities Edinburgh (above) and Glasgow. At large blending houses such as Clyde Bonding (opposite), malt whiskies are combined with grain whiskies. They are then left to "marry" for up to a year, a period known as the "honeymoon".

Medieval spires flank Princes Street in Edinburgh (page 124), where locals mingle in fashionable shops and cozy pubs like Kay's Bar (page 127).

In Glasgow, folks meet for a dram at the Pot Still (page 128), which offers over 170 different malt whiskies, one of the largest selections in Scotland.

the loading of packed cases onto container vehicles for despatch, is carried out automatically. One bottling line alone can bottle and pack up to 1,100 cases in an hour. One of the brands blended and bottled at the plant is Ballantines, a whisky known for many years in Canada. Another owned by the same company is Old Smuggler, which has always been one of the leading brands in Scandinavia.

At some stage in the process water is added to the whisky in order to "reduce" it to normal bottling strength. Both malt and grain whiskies come off the still at a much higher strength than the consumer would wish to drink and are reduced during blending and bottling. The usual strength of Scotch is eighty-six American proof, equivalent to forty-three percent alcohol by volume, although some single malts are bottled at slightly higher strengths. Strength in itself is not a virtue, and the addition of a little water enables the drinker to appreciate the flavour and aroma of the whisky better.

Both Edinburgh and Glasgow have surpassed Perth as centres of the Scotch whisky trade. Edinburgh is the centre of administration, law, and medicine in Scotland and one of the loveliest cities anywhere, a "profusion of eccentricities, this dream in masonry and living rock" as Robert Louis Stevenson described it. Edinburgh also has long associations with whisky, for it was in 1505 that the Guild of Surgeon Barbers was granted a monopoly in making and selling it in the city, no doubt because of the general belief in its medicinal properties.

The castle perched on a rocky crag dominates the city, brooding, it seems, over its turbulent history. It was King Malcolm III of Scotland, the last purely Gaelic king and conqueror of Macbeth, who built the original castle as his residence. The castle's oldest structure, the chapel that Malcolm built for his Saxon queen Margaret, dates back to 1076. Almost impregnable, Edinburgh Castle has only once been taken since the artillery of an English army destroyed its defenses in 1216. That was in 1314, when the Earl of Moray with thirty men scaled the north face of the rock and drove out the English, winning the castle back for Robert the Bruce.

A part of the esplanade, or parade ground, of the castle, where the famous Military Tattoo is held every summer, is officially Canadian territory. King Charles I, wishing to sell baronetcies to prospective settlers in Nova Scotia, had an Act of Parliament passed which required that anyone buying a baronetcy should be given a portion of Scottish soil, which then became Canadian.

The castle overlooks the Royal Mile which slopes gradually down to Holyrood House, the official palace of the sovereign when in Edinburgh. The medieval street is flanked on both sides by scores of narrow closes and wynds, or alleyways, many of them scenes of historic events. On each side, too, are buildings whose names proclaim their age and their history; St. Giles's Cathedral, the Tolbooth Kirk, the Signet Library, John Knox's House, Queen Mary's Bath House. One of the most picturesque of the closes is White Horse Close, named after a white palfrey of Mary, Queen of Scots, which much later gave its name to a well-known brand of Scotch whisky. All this is the Old Town, and on the other side of Princes Street stands the New Town, with its elegant Georgian square and crescents, the work of half-a-dozen famous architects including Robert Adam.

Many leading whisky companies now have offices in Edinburgh, and some have built bottling halls on the outskirts of the city. The Perth company of Arthur Bell and Sons built theirs a few years ago to bottle their whisky of the same name, and so did Hill Thomson and Company, owners of the Queen Anne brand. Macdonald and Muir, who own Glenmorangie Distillery, have bottled their Highland Queen blend in Edinburgh's ancient port of Leith for many years, and Donald Mackinlay's whisky is bottled not far from there.

There has always been spirited rivalry between Edinburgh and Glasgow. Glaswegians are apt to believe that Edinburgh folk put on a conceit which they do not merit, while the people of Edinburgh think of Glaswegians as earthy, combative, and unruly. Jack House, a well-known Scottish journalist, is reported to have said that in Edinburgh breeding is equated with good form, while in Glasgow breeding is regarded as good fun—a tongue-in-cheek observation which has at least an element of truth.

Glasgow has also been described as the finest Victorian city in Britain. Throughout the last century and the first half of the present one, its prosperity was based on shipbuilding, heavy en-gineering, and the steel industry. The city should not be thought of as an industrial wasteland, however, for the leaders of these great industries have endowed Glasgow with more and finer parks than any other comparable city and with art collections richer than any outside London. Another of its assets is that upon leaving it, in a few minutes one can be by Loch Lomond or in the Trossachs or along by the Clyde to the islands of the west.

The decline of the shipbuilding industry over the last thirty years or so led to a depression, and for a time Glasgow seemed to be infected with wasting and decay. This erosion has now passed, and a new spirit is emerging as its problems are tackled with the energy and imagination for which the Scot has always been renowned.

Scotch has always had a strong presence in Glasgow, not only in the pubs and bars. Some of the oldest companies are based there. William Teacher, the son of a woman who worked in a spinning mill near Glasgow, joined her in the mill at the age of seven. He married Agnes McDonald in 1834 and worked in her mother's grocery business, which had taken out a liquor license. Soon, under his direction, it became a wholesale wine and spirit merchants and began running Dram shops in the city. By 1861 William Teacher and Sons had eighteen Dram shops in the city, austere establishments in which a customer could buy a dram of whisky for threepence, drink it, and be on his way. Smoking was prohibited and so was treating, so one would have found none of

the cheerful camaraderie typical of a modern pub. At about that time the firm moved into the blended whisky trade, and in 1874 it established itself in offices in St. Enoch Square on a site which its head office still occupies. Teacher's Highland Cream was soon one of the leading brands of Scotch in the United Kingdom.

As we have seen, most of the major whisky companies started as wine merchants who expanded into selling blended Scotch whisky. To do this they bought the single whiskies they needed for their blends from distillers, and later, to safeguard their supplies, most of them bought or built distilleries of their own. One exception to this trend was William Grant and Sons, the company of Sandy Grant Gordon, one of the "highlanders" whom I had met on their way to Skye. Grants were distillers in the north who expanded into blended whisky, moved to offices in Glasgow, and built a bottling hall in Paisley, just outside the city.

Another firm which made the journey from the north was Chivas Brothers, originally a licensed grocers in Aberdeen. The firm had been founded in 1801 by a William Edward, who was joined by James Chivas in 1838. In the 1890s the firm began to become involved in the whisky business; later, after they became a wholly-owned subsidiary of the Seagram Company, they achieved a spectacular success with their deluxe brand Chivas Regal, now one of the leading prestige brands of Scotch. To satisfy the demand for the brand, the firm built large, modern blending and bottling halls near Glasgow.

The rapid growth in the popularity of Scotch in the period following the mid-1950s has been phenomenal, and nothing like it has been known in the history of drink and drinking. Everyone began drinking Scotch. To offer it at diplomatic receptions in embassies wherever they might be became *de rigeur*. It replaced champagne as the fashionable drink in night clubs and became the largest selling item in duty free stores at every international airport. Countries like Japan, where before the war it was scarcely known, became leading markets for Scotch, while soon the French were drinking more Scotch than their own Cognac.

Whisky firms who owned or developed brands which had a special appeal in major markets did particularly well during this period. One such firm was Berry Brothers and Rudd of St. James's Street in the most fashionable part of London. Berry Brothers are one of the oldest and most highly regarded wine merchants in London, having been in business at the same address for more than 250 years.

A visit to their old oak-panelled shop is an experience to be cherished and, whether you go to order a case of Château Latour or a miniature bottle of Scotch, you will be welcomed and treated with consideration and courtesy. From old prints and invoices on display, you can see that the list of the firm's clients is a piece of history in itself, with names like Napoleon III, Byron, Beau Brummell, Robert Peel, the French Rothschilds, Melba, Alexander Woolcott, Laurence Olivier, and scores

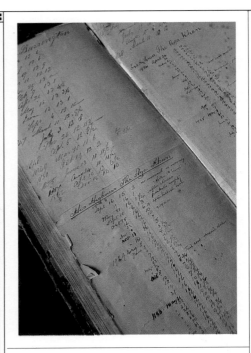

The oldest and most highly-regarded of London's wine and whisky merchants, Berry Brothers and Rudd (opposite) have welcomed customers to their elegant, oak-panelled offices in St. James's Street for over two centuries. On the walls hang old prints and invoices to clients such as Napoleon III, Beau Brummell, and Sir Laurence Olivier. After making their selections, renowned patrons often sat to be weighed in the shop's great scales. The weight book (above), which dates back to 1765, can still be seen today.

Berry Brothers and Rudd began selling their own blends before World War I, and in 1923 they introduced an elegant, pale-coloured whisky called Cutty Sark. An immediate success, Cutty Sark remains one of the most popular blended Scotches in the world.

of others. A feature of the shop is the great scales in which famous people have sat to be weighed, their weights recorded in one of the bound volumes which date back to 1765.

The firm was selling their own brands of Scotch before the First World War, and in 1923 the partners decided to bottle a special blend for the export trade, particularly America. The blend was one of high-quality whiskies, light in flavour and free of any colouring. A well-known Scottish artist, James McBey, designed a label for the new blend, which had been given the name "Cutty Sark". The Cutty Sark was a famous clipper, the fastest sailing ship afloat, which had once sailed 363 miles in one day.

The ship's name, for a reason which no one has ever explained to me, came from Robert Burns' famous poem *Tam o'Shanter* and means a short chemise. The whisky Cutty Sark was an immediate success and soon became one of the brand leaders in the United States and throughout the world.

Another great firm of London wine merchants to enter the Scotch whisky trade with outstanding success was Justerini and Brooks. Giacomo Justerini had come to England in 1749 when an Italian opera singer he was in love with was given a contract to sing in London. In the 1880s the firm became one of the first London wine merchants to establish their own blend of Scotch whisky. Today J & B Rare is one of the leading brands of Scotch in the world and, although perhaps the name Justerini has nothing to do with it, a special favourite among Italians.

In order to meet the growing demand for Scotch in the 1960s, many distilleries were expanded by equipping them with additional stills, and some new distilleries were built. Since Scotch has to be matured for at least three years, or four if it is to be sold in the United States, stocks of whisky have to be laid down to meet likely sales several years ahead. Often these stocks are held at distilleries in traditional warehouses—long, low buildings in which the casks may be stacked on top of each other, not more than three-high. In recent years companies have been building more modern warehouses with racking in which casks can be stored in several rows, making handling and inspection much easier.

Scotch whisky is now exported to almost every country in the world, including Moslem countries, and more than 190 are listed in official export records. The annual value of these exports is currently in excess of two billion dollars, and while it is difficult to calculate the value of stocks, since the whisky will be of different ages and stages of maturation, their saleable value must certainly be more than the entire gold and dollar reserves of the United Kingdom.

One might reflect on the old adage that from little acorns spring mighty oaks and be tempted to think that Scotland owes to little aphids all the prosperity which Scotch has brought. That would not be true. Phylloxera certainly played its part in starting the development of Scotch as a worldwide drink, but the ultimate success would not have been achieved without the energy and imagination of salesmen who took it around the world, and the dedication and integrity of distillers who stayed at home and maintained its traditions. For in the final instance, the success of Scotch is dependent, not on luck, but on its merits as a drink of a unique flavour and unsurpassed quality.

A Drink for All Seasons

During one of my visits to Speyside, Evan Cattanach took me as his guest to a Burns Night Supper in Fraserburgh. Fraserburgh is a fishing port on the bleak north-east coast of Scotland, never a romantic place even in summer, and in January grey and drab. The Alexandra Hotel, in which the supper was held, is an ordinary commercial hotel which tries its best but gives the impression that its best was several years ago. That night though, the scene in the hotel ballroom was elegant and colourful. More than two hundred members of the Fraserburgh Burns Club and their guests had gathered for the supper, less than half of them in tuxedos and the rest wearing kilts, with the different tartans, patterned in green, red, yellow, and blue, affording a fine contrast to the white of the tablecloths and the silver of the cutlery.

After supper a local schoolmaster, a talented after-dinner speaker, would give the address "The Immortal Memory of Robert Burns". Evan would then sing for us *"My Luv is like a red, red rose"* and perhaps *"Flow gently sweet Afton, among thy green braes"*, a fiddler would play, and another member, unless forcibly restrained, would recite the full 224 lines of Burns's long poem *Tam o' Shanter*.

Before that though, there would be ceremonies to enjoy. When we had drunk our soup, the club's piper piped in the haggis. The chef carried it on a silver dish, following the piper round the room and up to the top table

where he placed it before Mr. Charles Thomson who, knife in hand, addressed it:

> *Fair Fa' your honest, sonsie face,*
> *Great Chieftain o' the Puddin-race,*
> *Aboon them a' ye tak your place,*
> *Painch, tripe or thairm,*
> *Weel are ye wordy of a grace,*
> *As lang's my arm.*

Often when haggis is addressed at a dinner only the first verse of Burns's ode is recited, but that night we were given all eight verses. At the end of them Charles Thomson raised his knife and cut deeply into the haggis. Three glasses of whisky stood on the table in front of him. He handed one to the piper—the traditional way in which one "pays the piper"—one to the chef, and picked up the third himself. The three men raised their glasses for the time-honored Gaelic toast for good health—*slainte vhar*—and then each of them downed his whisky in a single swallow.

Drinking Scotch that way, in a single draught, is not to be recommended. Quite apart from other considerations, it does not allow you the time to appreciate the subtlety of its flavour. Scotch is a drink one should linger over and enjoy, but at a Burns Night Supper or any other occasion where haggis is served in the traditional manner, it is more than just a drink, it is a ritual, part of the ceremony. To down it in one swallow is in keeping with the macho image of the piper as a warrior, and the man who addresses it and the chef are obliged to show that they can match him.

How then should one drink Scotch? Englishmen and even some Scots are apt to say that it should be drunk with an equal quantity of cold, spring water and never in any other way. Those who claim this do not really know Scotch whisky, nor do they understand the wide range of pleasures it can offer. And those who persist in drinking it only with water, regardless of the occasion, the locale, or the climate are depriving themselves of many enjoyable drinking experiences.

A year or two back I was in Dallas, staying at the Mansion on Turtle Creek, a hotel with standards of comfort and service that would be hard to match. In the early evening I went into the bar and found it full of young men and women, enjoying a drink after work or on their way to dine either in the hotel's restaurant or one of the other many good restaurants in Dallas.

A lone Scottish businessman, unmistakable for his accent, arrived, found a table, and asked the exceptionally pretty young waitress for a Scotch, ordering it, as anyone who knows his whisky should, by brand name. Then, no doubt because he had experienced difficulty in having Scotch served the way he wanted in some American bars, he added with special emphasis that he wanted no ice in the Scotch and would like some water to be brought to him separately. What he was afraid of was that if the barman added water to the Scotch he would put in too much. What he was served was a Scotch without rocks and a glass of iced water on the side. I watched with little sympathy as he tried to add water to the Scotch from the glass, holding back the ice cubes with his fingers and spilling a good deal of it on the table and some on his pants.

Burns Night is the annual celebration of the birthday of Robert Burns. A lover of whisky—and, ironically, a former Excise Officer—Burns is known worldwide as the whisky poet. Readings from his works are punctuated by toasts and raised drams, and revelers always end a Burns Night Supper singing "Auld Lang Syne", which was written by Burns.

The main course at these events is a haggis, a type of sausage made from lamb and oatmeal, which is escorted into the dining hall by a kilt-clad bagpiper and addressed by the host. Bill Forbes, President of the St. Andrew's Society of Washington, D.C., toasts the haggis (opposite) at a 1989 Burns Night Supper.

❖

Previous page: Patrick Cruickshank of J & P Cruickshank in Fochabers proudly offers his world-class Scottish haggis.

The moral of the story has nothing to do with language or the difficulty of communication even among those who speak the same tongue. Rather it is that lovers of Scotch, no matter what their personal preferences, should take time to reflect on why it is that people in different parts of the world drink Scotch in different ways.

My godfather left Perth while I was still a boy and spent most of his working life on tea plantations in Assam and later, Ceylon. He loved his whisky but, once in the East, always drank it with soda. Almost everyone in that part of the world did the same, and if asked to articulate the reason for this, he might have said rather vaguely that undiluted spirits were in some imprecise way not good for one in tropical climates, or muttered something about having to replace the body water which was lost through perspiring. The real reason, I suggest very seriously, is that although the flavour of any particular make or brand of Scotch must be constant, its taste on the palate does change in different climates, on different occasions, and at different times. And that is why in the tea plantations of Assam, a *chota peg* of Scotch with soda is what the palate appreciates most, just as in Dallas the oil millionaires and yuppies like their Scotch on the rocks. Our Scot in the Mansion on Turtle Creek, had he been imaginative enough to try it that way, might well have found that he preferred it.

Scotch whisky is, in fact, a versatile drink, adaptable to almost any climate and any occasion. Those who are fortunate enough to be invited for a day's fishing in one of the great salmon rivers of Scotland should take a flask of Scotch with them, for one cannot be sure that the gillie will bring enough for two, although in distilling country he well might. After standing up to your thighs in water for some hours, you will probably prefer to take your whisky as it comes from the bottle, with nothing added.

The same would be true for those who play the Scotsman's game of curling on an outdoor rink. A unique event in the Scottish curling calendar is the Grand Match between teams of curlers, one representing the north of Scotland and the other, the south. At the beginning of the winter, the Royal Caledonian Curling Club, the governing authority of curling in Scotland, nominates the two teams, each made up of three hundred or more "rinks" of four players. Each side will know the name of the rink which it will curl against and will also know that the match will be played on one of three nominated lochs. What makes the event unique—and very rare—is that it only takes place if one of the three lochs freezes hard enough to give ice that will support the weight of some twenty-four hundred curlers, their curling stones and other equipment, the many supporters, and, of course, the whisky they take to drink with their lunch as the day unfolds.

John Grant of Glenfarclas Distillery described the scene of the last Grand Match, which was held in the winter of 1979. Three days previously the curlers had been alerted that the match might take place if the freeze continued. On the evening

before, announcements were made on television and radio that the match was definitely on. The next morning hundreds of curlers, easily recognized by the brooms and stones they were carrying, could be seen standing by the roads, waiting for friends to pick them up and drive them to Lake Menteith where the match was to be played. The ice had been marked out, and soon twenty-four hundred curlers, all of whom had been asked to wear something tartan, were waiting for the signal to start. It was given by Lord Elgin, the President of the Caledonian Curling Club, who arrived in a helicopter and fired a cannon at eleven o'clock.

The match continued until about four in the afternoon. Scotch is the perfect drink for a curling match, especially when it is held outdoors, providing exactly the stimulus and the comforting warmth that curlers need on an invigorating winter's day. Just in case those curling in the match might not have brought enough whisky with them, William Teacher and Sons of Glasgow had very generously brought a hogshead holding more than a hundred gallons, which was positioned at the edge of the lake. By the end of the day the cask was in danger of falling through the ice, not because of its weight, but because the passage of so many hundreds of pairs of feet, as curlers and spectators came and went to draw a dram, had begun to melt the ice around the cask. All those who were at Lake Menteith that day have fond memories of that Grand Match and will be hoping that they may be fortunate enough to see another played in their lifetime.

Cocktails are generally considered a relatively modern invention, modern that is when measured against the centuries-old history of Scotch whisky. In reality, though, it is only the name that is modern. For as long as anyone can recall, Scotch has been mixed with other drinks in a variety of pleasing forms. The Whisky Toddy is one of the oldest examples, a combination of Scotch, lemon juice, and honey, with perhaps a stick of cinnamon, served hot and preferably in a silver mug. The Toddy is a delightful drink which is always looking for a common cold or even just a suspicion of a winter's chill to provide an excuse for drinking it. Equally traditional is the Whisky Mac, a combination of Scotch and green ginger wine. Ginger wine is not available everywhere, but if you can get hold of a bottle of Crabbie's, made by a firm who also makes an excellent blended Scotch, treasure it and lock it up in a cupboard or, if you are one of those ascetic characters who has convinced himself that a drink should only be medicinal, in your medicine chest.

In the Caledonian Club in London a favourite drink has always been a Chairman's Special, simply named but rich in the pleasure it gives. A combination of malt whisky and Drambuie, the proportions of each drink should be varied to suit individual taste. Many people like equal quantities of the whisky and the liqueur, but I have always found that combination too sweet for my taste and prefer to mix two-thirds Scotch whisky with one-third Drambuie. Drambuie is made to a secret recipe which obviously includes honey and herbs;

it is labelled as a liqueur from the Isle of Skye, specially-prepared for Prince Charles Edward. The drink is often called a Rusty Nail and many ingenious and implausible explanations have been put forward for why that name was chosen, but I have never met anyone who could speak with real authority on the matter.

Two other traditional drinks which were being mixed in Scotland long before the name cocktail was invented are Het Pint and Atholl Brose. Het Pint is made of whisky, mild ale, beaten eggs, sugar, and grated nutmeg. It is served hot from kettles on Hogmanay, the last day of the old year and a holiday always celebrated in Scotland with reckless abandon. Atholl Brose is an unusual combination of oatmeal, honey, and Scotch, a potent drink named after an early Duke of Atholl, who in 1475 captured his great enemy the Earl of Ross by pouring the brose into a well from which the Earl was known to draw water. The Earl drank the brose and while sleeping off its effects was seized and made prisoner. Making the drink successfully appears to me to require an inherent skill, in much the same way as a few talented cooks can make good pastry effortlessly, while scores of others, including myself, are fated always to pull out of the baking oven either sad, soggy messes or tablets of stone which would have served Moses well. The textbooks say that you should mix oatmeal with water, put it through a strainer, mix the liquid with honey, add a quart of Scotch, and, after bottling, leave it for at least two days before serving it.

All these are traditional Scottish drinks, and traditionalists would be affronted if one called them cocktails. The Scot is a cautious fellow, conservative by nature whatever his political leanings, and it was some time after the arrival of cocktails and flappers and the Charleston before daring souls in Scotland began mixing their whisky with strange foreign drinks. It may even have been a French barman who mixed the first Scotch cocktail, for during *la belle epoque*, the days when Paris was the centre of the world and rich American heiresses crossed the Atlantic to marry French princes and *comtes*, the horse-racing fraternity at Longchamps were fond of a drink made of Scotch, cider, and Angostura bitters. They called it a Stone Fence, which suggests that one had to negotiate it with care.

A cocktail which has been drunk in Scotland for many years is Purple Heather. I was introduced to it at St. Andrew's, when I had been playing golf in a meeting arranged by John Walker and Sons. Golf and Scotch have always gone together, and among the whisky men at that meeting were two Walker Cup players, three Scottish internationals, and at least five other scratch-handicap players. One of them was David Blair, managing director of James Buchanan and Sons. In the bar after our two rounds on the Old Course, David told a story against himself. A few years previously, at an age not far short of fifty, he had been chosen to play for Great Britain against the United States in the Walker Cup. He had been in brilliant form that season, but it was still a remarkable achieve-

Whisky goes hand in hand with many popular sports. At St. Andrew's, the world's oldest and most prestigious golf course, members often finish off a round of golf with a dram in the clubhouse (below).

The Spey is Scotland's greatest salmon river, and it attracts fishermen from around the world. But an angler cannot just walk up to the river's edge and drop in his line. Rather, he must rent space along the river—at very steep rates—and hire an experienced gillie (page 137) to see that he gets the best catch.

ment to have been selected for the Walker Cup at his age. The match was being played in the States that year and, knowing that the weather was likely to be warm and sunny, David had a new pair of white plus twos specially made for the occasion and thought he looked rather well in them. On the morning of the match, the American team, some of them hideously young—they included a very young Jack Nicklaus—were changing, and David was in the changing room out of sight but not out of earshot. He overheard one of the Americans ask another whom he had drawn to play.

"I don't know the name of the guy," the other replied, "but he's an elderly gentleman in white knickerbockers."

I often drink Purple Heather after golf, not in the belief that some of David Blair's golfing skill will be passed on to me, but because it is pleasant to taste, easy to make, long, light, and refreshing. Simply add a little crème de cassis, the French drink made from black currants which is used with white wine to make the aperitif Kir, to a jigger of Scotch, top it up with club soda, and add ice and a slice of lemon.

Once while on a visit to the States I was persuaded by James Bruxner, the managing director of Justerini and Brooks, to try

what he called a Bloody Joseph, which was, in effect, a Bloody Mary made with Scotch instead of vodka. He assured me that Scotch added a depth, a rich quality not to be found in a conventional Bloody Mary, and in spite of my scepticism, I realized at once that this was true. Not caring much for the cocktail's name, I rechristened it a Bannockburn, after the famous battle in 1314 at which Robert the Bruce with a few hundred Scots annihilated an English army. A museum has been built on the site of the battle just outside the town of Stirling. Scotch and tomato juice, I feel, are appropriate symbols for the Scottish spirit which triumphed over English blood on that historic day.

Discovering the Bannockburn started me reflecting on the nature of cocktails. A perfect cocktail, surely, should be one in which the diverse and often contrasting flavours of the ingredients should meld together and produce a drink which has a distinctive and completely different flavour of its own, just as in a perfect culinary dish every ingredient contributes to the final taste. If this is true, then Scotch is an ideal drink to use. Of course, there are many cocktails in which fruit juices, syrups, and fortified wines are added to a largely tasteless spirit like gin or vodka, but it always seems to me that in these cocktails the spirit is being used simply to provide alcohol and makes little contribution to the character of the drink.

Creating a new cocktail requires skill and experience. An amateur may play the barman with the assortment of drinks he has in his den,

experimenting by using varying proportions of each, aiming perhaps at an exotic colour in the final mixture and kidding himself that he is about to launch a thrilling new cocktail on an astonished world. More often than not his creation will be all but undrinkable. A professional barman works in a different and more scientific way. He understands drinks and knows from experience which ones he can mix with each other and which are hopelessly incompatible.

One leading Scottish bartender who has shown a special skill in creating cocktails with Scotch is Buchanan Aitken. Buckie, as he is known to his friends, has his own lounge bar and restaurant in the small village of Croftamie, not far from Loch Lomond, where besides his cocktails one is offered a selection of the best malt whiskies. He believes that cocktails can be mixed to suit every mood and every occasion; short, astringent appetizers to liven the taste buds; rich, creamy after-dinner drinks— "digestifs" as the French call them—and long, cool drinks for summer. A favourite of mine among his creations is Golden Glory, made with Scotch, sherry, and dry vermouth; another is Scotch Bounty, an intriguing combination of Scotch, Malibu, and crème de cacao. Buckie's Brose is far removed from the Duke of Atholl's Brose and is based on Scotch and a coffee liqueur with honey and a sprinkling of oatmeal on top.

The increasing popularity of Scotch and the growing interest in cocktails have led many internationally known bartenders to devise new Scotch cocktails. One of the most notable and

unusual is the 21 Salute created by Will Higgins of New York's famous 21 Club; it combines Scotch, apricot brandy, and blackberry brandy, with a lemon-lime sour mix. James Kelly has created Scottish Summer. James works at the Four Seasons, a favourite restaurant of smart and affluent New Yorkers and his cocktail is relatively simple, made up of Scotch, Lochan Ora, and lemon juice. Even the Russian Tea Room, probably better known for a certain white spirit, has been seduced by the vogue for Scotch cocktails, and bartender Tim Reid has devised Smoked Scotch, in which a splash of peach schnapps and another of Cointreau are used. I was intrigued by the name,

wondering how Tim had managed to produce a drink smokier than Scotch itself. Then I learnt that the smoke is not in the flavour, but rises from the surface of the cocktail after it has been poured and a small amount of warm water added to a very small container of dry ice at the centre of the cocktail.

❖

Whisky has always been part of the Scot's staple diet and at one time it would be drunk with every meal. In one of his novels the Scottish author Tobias George Smollett describes a typical Scottish breakfast of two hundred years ago; boiled

Bartender Tim Reid of the Russian Tea Room shows off his famous Smoked Scotch (opposite).

Scots have been combining whisky with other ingredients for centuries. The Atholl Brose named for an early Duke of Atholl, is a cocktail of Scotch, oatmeal, and honey. By increasing the amount of oatmeal the cocktail becomes a dessert eaten with a spoon (below). Tulchan Lodge's Nutty Bumble Whisky Cake is another dessert that features Scotch (page 147).

❖

Previous page: New Yorkers gather for Scotch cocktails at Keen's Chop House in Manhattan.

eggs, cheese, ham, venison pasties, oatcakes, honey, and a stone bottle of whisky.

Usually Scotch is used to enhance the flavour of food, but sometimes to disguise it. Once the organizers of the annual film festival in Cannes decided to hold a Scottish day. Films set in Scotland were screened, the St. Andrew's Cross—the flag of Scotland—was flown on buildings and displayed together with a wealth of tartan material in the cinema, in bars, and in shops. The pipes and drums of a Scottish regiment paraded through the streets, and as a finale, a Scottish banquet was held in the ballroom of the casino, with a menu of cock-a-leekie, Aberdeen Angus beef, and, of course, haggis.

I found myself seated at the banquet next to Bertrand, a journalist acknowledged to be the leading writer on food and drink in France. When the haggis was piped in, he asked me to explain how it was made. I told him that it was the liver, heart, lungs, and other unmentionable parts of a sheep, mixed with oatmeal and cooked in the lining of a sheep's stomach. I was rather proud that I even knew the French term for the dish, "panse de brebis farcie". Bertrand listened attentively and then said, *"Ah, un saucisson."* He was right, of course; although I had never thought of haggis as a sausage, that is exactly what it is, Scotland's favourite sausage.

Haggis is a dish whose taste and quality vary enormously. Scottish housewives have made a reputation simply on their skill at turning out a good haggis. They do it once for the village Burns Night Supper and then are invited to cook it every year for as long as they can still wield a chopping knife. A good haggis can be superb, moist and spicy and appetizing. Equally well a poor haggis can be dry and musty, or tasteless and hard to swallow. Our haggis at the Cannes film festival belonged definitely in the second category. An old hand at haggis, good and otherwise, I knew how to deal with it. Everyone had been given a glass of Scotch to drink with the haggis; I poured mine all over it. Bertrand, watching me,

did the same. I looked at him as he tasted the first mouthful.

"Well?"

"The dish is not distinguished, my friend, but—" he paused, smacking his lips, "the sauce is magnificent."

One does not have to pour Scotch over one's food to enjoy it with a meal. Those who take it with a meal usually dilute it with plenty of water or ice, making a long drink, a "light" Scotch some people call it. In this form it goes particularly well with the strongly flavoured dishes associated with Indian, Chinese, and Mexican cuisines.

Scotch is also often used as an ingredient in cooking. Highland Prawns is a dish from the west of Scotland which I first tasted on Skye and which, despite its simple ingredients—prawns, potatoes, onion, a little cream, and whisky—has a flavour difficult to describe and equally difficult to resist. I have tried cooking it without the whisky and found it far less appetizing.

In the nineteenth century the Cleikim Club in Edinburgh had a recipe for lobster which was cooked with whisky and almonds, then served with bananas. Another dish from the same period is Tweed Kettle, made with salmon, shallots, and cream. It is not only fish though, that is improved by cooking in whisky. I recall having roast chicken with honey, almonds, and whisky at Prestonfield House, one of Edinburgh's best restaurants, which was superb, and Skirlie, a traditional stuffing for poultry, is made with oatmeal, onion, herbs, and whisky. Black Bun, a type of rich cake eaten at

Hogmanay, needs whisky to give it the best flavour and consistency, and is often accompanied by a draught of Het Pint.

Scotch is sometimes used in dishes that are flambéed, or flamed. Personally I feel that setting a dish alight after pouring brandy, rum, or Scotch over it may give a spectacular effect that often appeals to inexperienced diners, but adds little to the flavour. Crêpes Suzette is a classic flambé dish, considered a must for every foreigner who dines in Maxim's in Paris's Rue Royale. Maxim's is another legacy from *la belle epoque*, arguably the most famous restaurant in the world and so popular among affluent visitors that one doorman there grew rich enough on his tips to buy a château in the Pyrenees.

A French friend once took me to Maxim's and pressed me to try the Crêpes Suzette. I agreed, but persuaded the *maître d'hôtel* to have them made not with orange Curaçao or Grand Marnier, but with Scotch. The result was a great improvement, not nearly so sweet as the more conventional dessert and a pleasant way to finish a meal. Only later did I discover there already was a pancake dish made with Scotch, called Crêpes Mary Stuart in memory of the sad, sweet Scottish Queen.

People new to Scotch often find if difficult to choose from among the different types and brands that are available. They may ask themselves how closely price is equated with quality. Are single malts and the more expensive premium or deluxe

Scotches best suited for drinking only on special occasions? What type of Scotch should one buy for making cocktails or for use in cooking? Is the age of a Scotch any guarantee of quality?

One cannot repeat too emphatically that taste is purely subjective and the choice of a Scotch must therefore always be a matter for individual preference. A brand which appeals to one person may seem bland and uninteresting or too pungent to another. All one can give is general guidance on what a drinker should look for and what he has a right to expect in Scotch whisky. In most good bars and liquor stores you will find two kinds of Scotch, blended whisky and malt whisky. Blended Scotch comes in three varieties; premium or deluxe blends, bottled-in-Scotland blends, and those that are shipped in bulk and bottled in the States. Most of the Scotch malt whiskies that are on sale are single malts, that is the unblended whisky distilled in one distillery and normally labelled with its name.

Recently a number of what are known in Scotland as "vatted malts" have also been put on the market. A vatted malt is, in effect, a blend of malt whiskies from a number of different distilleries, with no grain whisky at all. Vatted malts are labelled with a name of some place or region of Scotland, or one suggesting Scottish origin, but the label does not always make this clear. Anyone who knows the names of the hundred-odd distilleries in Scotland will recognize a single malt by the name of the distillery from which it comes, but not everyone has this know-

ledge. The best advice one can give is to look for the description "single" on the label.

Premium brands of Scotch are usually a good deal more expensive than standard brands, and some may wonder why this is so. Part of the reason is age. As I mentioned before, all Scotch whisky must be matured in oak casks for a minimum of three years, and all Scotch sold in the States is at least four years old. But age is expensive to acquire. The maturation of whisky involves a slow evaporation during which something like two-and-a-half percent of the whisky is lost every year, drifting up into the heavens, "the angels' share", they say. Upwards of one-fifth of a cask of whisky will be lost in this way if it is allowed to mature for twelve years, and there is also, of course, the cost of keeping money tied up for all that time.

What is the best age for a whisky? One cannot be dogmatic in answering, for although in general the older the whisky the better it should be, whisky from some distilleries matures more quickly than others and, having reached its peak, does not improve significantly no matter how long it is left in the cask. One may assume that in well-known standard brands of Scotch all the constituent single whiskies will have been matured for between five and seven years. Premium blends are always older; in recent times many of them have been bottled at twelve years and state so on the label. Single malt whiskies may be bottled at different ages—seven, ten, twelve, and fifteen years are all common—and the same malt may be matured for different periods of time to suit tastes. If an age is given on the label, every whisky in the blend must have been matured for that time; averaging is not allowed and this is strictly controlled.

At one time many people believed that whisky should never be left to mature for more than fifteen years, in the belief that whisky did not improve beyond that age and, instead, was likely to deteriorate. Then in 1952 Chivas Brothers exploded the theory when, to commemorate the coronation of the Queen, they produced Royal Salute, a twenty-one-year-old blend. The blend, elegantly presented in a Spode china flagon which was wrapped in a velvet pouch, was, as the French say, a "succes fou". Protocol in using names of royalty or the royal coat of arms is very strict in Britain, but Chivas were allowed to use the royal coat of arms on the flagons, but only during the year of the coronation; afterwards they reverted to using the company's coat of arms. If by any chance you have one of the original 1952 flagons, treasure it whether it still holds whisky or not, for it will be a rare and valuable collector's piece.

By law Scotch must be aged for at least three years, but most of the best whiskies are older, such as those displayed on the bar of the Minmore House (opposite), the original home of the founder of The Glenlivet Distillery. Sometimes the age of a whisky is important for reasons other than its flavour. In 1982, Strathisla introduced a vatted malt in honor of the wedding of Prince Charles and Lady Diana Spencer (below); it contained two single malts, one from 1948, the year of his birth, and one from 1961, the year of hers.

❖

Following page: Christian Orr-Ewing and his dog, Hernia, have a whisky on the rocks at Kay's Bar in Edinburgh.

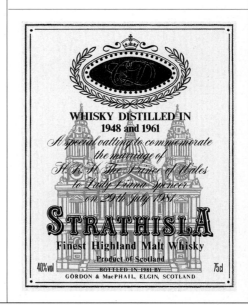

Since that time at least one company has put a fifty-year-old Scotch on sale, and recently Allan Shiach of Macallan Distillers went one better. He auctioned off a bottle of sixty-year-old Macallan with a label specially designed by a well-known artist; it was knocked down for more than $10,000, which must surely be a record for a single bottle of Scotch whisky.

Most people will choose the type and price of Scotch to suit the occasion when it is to be drunk or the purpose to which it will be put, but here again it is a matter of individual preference. I like to drink a single malt or premium Scotch after a meal, served in a snifter glass so I can savour its aroma and bouquet. Standard blends should be used for cocktails unless the recipe specifically calls for a malt. Bottled-in-America blends are what I use in cooking.

Remember that Scotch does not mature or improve in any way once it has been bottled. Many connoiseurs believe that if it is left too long in a bottle Scotch will begin to take on "bottle flavour". I have never found anyone who could define bottle flavour, but I must concede that after a period of time in a bottle, whisky seems to lose its freshness and some of its character. So if you are hoarding those few fingers of a fine old single malt which your mother-in-law with a burst of generosity gave you five Christmasses ago in the hope that it will improve, don't waste your time. Finish it off and go out and buy another bottle.

All Scots know that whisky is a versatile drink because ever since they learnt the art of distillation it has been part of their life, their culture, and their history. In the long struggle against English oppression it fortified them both on the battlefield and when, unarmed, they were being hunted down and slaughtered mercilessly by redcoat soldiers. In the Highlands, whisky gave them comfort when they were evicted from their lands and herded on ships to be sent into exile. It became a symbol of hospitality in every home however humble, with a jug or flask of whisky always ready to welcome guests with a dram. Scotch is an indispensable part of every celebration—christenings, weddings, and wakes, just as it has always had a role in every ceremony and social rite.

Scots, women as well as men, drink it neat or with water when they fish, shoot, curl, or play golf. In Glasgow, shipwrights and steel melters like a "half and half", a whisky and a beer. In Edinburgh, lawyers and accountants sip it politely and call it "a small refreshment". In pubs throughout Scotland, men, as well as women, drink it with lemonade, a fizzy drink not unlike Seven Up. They drink Scotch to ward off influenza or to soften the aches and pains of rheumatism. They lace their tea and coffee with it, and drink it last thing at night to promote sleep. For centuries they have drunk their whisky with every meal and cooked with it too. So when the cocktail arrived to bring sophistication to drinking, they found no difficulty in devising hundreds more ways to enjoy it. With hindsight, when Holinshed said "Trulie it is a sovereigne liquor" he might well have added, "and verily it is a drink for all seasons".

Scotland's Whisky Trail

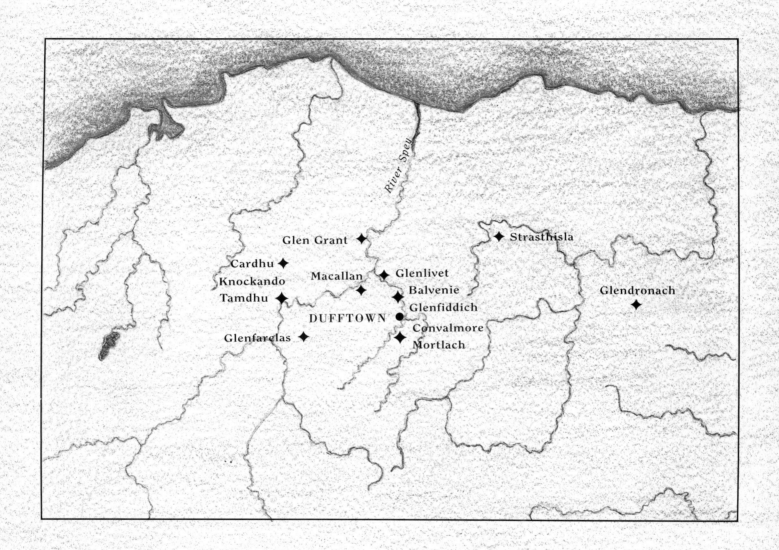

Glenmorangie

Wester Ross

SKYE

Talisker

INVERNESS

Loch Ness

THE WHISKY TRAIL

Blair Castle

Edradour

DUNDEE

PERTH

ST. ANDREW'S

Loch Lomond

JURA

Bunnahabhain
Caol Ila
ISLAY
Bruichladdich   Bowmore
Ardbeg
Laphroaig   Lagavulin

EDINBURGH

Glenkinchie

GLASGOW

KILMARNOCK

Scotch Whisky Recipes

TRADITIONAL SCOTTISH DRINKS

ATHOLL BROSE

4 tablespoons oatmeal
4 dessert spoons clear honey
Scotch whisky
Water

Mix the oatmeal with enough water to make a thick paste. Allow the mixture to sit for forty-five minutes, then pass it through a fine strainer, pressing the oatmeal down with a spoon. Mix the liquid with the honey, pour it into a quart bottle, top up with whisky, and set aside for at least two days. Shake well before serving.

HET PINT

2 pints Scotch ale
1/2 pint Scotch whisky
4 ounces sugar
Nutmeg, cloves, cinnamon

Bring the ale to the boil, pour in the whisky, and add spices to taste. Serve hot in tankards.

RUSTY NAIL

1 measure Scotch whisky
1/2 measure Drambuie

Mix the whisky and the Drambuie well, preferably in a snifter glass, and serve with or without ice.

COCKTAILS FROM SCOTLAND

PURPLE HEATHER

1 ounce Scotch whisky
2 teaspoons crème de cassis
Club soda

Stir Scotch and cassis in a highball glass with ice, then top up with soda.

ROYAL MILE

1 ounce Scotch whisky
1 ounce blue Curaçao
1 ounce Sirop de Orgeat
4 ounces orange juice
Dash of egg white
Dash of fresh lemon juice

Combine the ingredients in a shaker with ice, shake vigorously, and pour into tall glass. Garnish with a slice of orange, and serve with a straw.

BUCKIE'S BROSE

1 ounce Scotch whisky
1 ounce Kahlua
1 ounce double cream
1 teaspoon heather honey

Combine all ingredients in a shaker with ice, shake, and strain into a cocktail glass. Sprinkle with toasted oatmeal before serving.
Created by Buchanan Aitken
The Wayfarers

BANNOCKBURN

5 ounces tomato juice
1 ounce Scotch whisky
2 dashes of Worcestershire sauce

Combine all ingredients, and stir well. Add ice, and serve with a slice of lemon. Tabasco sauce may be added, or used instead of the Worcestershire.

SCOTCH BOUNTY

1 ounce Scotch whisky
1 ounce Malibu
1 ounce white crème de cacao
4 ounces unsweetened orange juice
Dash of egg white
Dash of grenadine

Combine all ingredients in a shaker with ice, shake vigorously, and pour into a tall glass. Garnish with a slice of orange and a cherry, and serve with a straw.

ROBERT BURNS COCKTAIL

1 1/2 ounces Scotch whisky
1/2 ounce Italian vermouth
Dash of Pernod
Dash of orange bitters

Stir all ingredients with ice cubes, and strain into a chilled cocktail glass.

STONE FENCE

1 measure Scotch whisky
Angostura bitters
Cider

Pour the Scotch and two dashes of bitters into an ice-filled highball glass. Top up with cider, stirring all the time.

FLYING SCOTSMAN

2 ounces Scotch whisky
1 ounce sweet vermouth
2 dashes Angostura bitters
l sugar cube

Place the sugar cube in the bottom of a cocktail glass, then drop the bitters over the sugar. Pour in the whisky and vermouth, and stir.

COCKTAILS FROM THE BIG APPLE

21 SALUTE
1 ounce Scotch whisky
1/2 ounce apricot brandy
1/2 ounce blackberry brandy
1/2 ounce lemon/lime sour mix
Dash of grenadine for colouring

In a blender half-filled with ice, blend all the ingredients until completely slushed. Serve in a large, chilled cocktail glass, garnished with a cherry or an orange slice.
Created by Will Higgins
The 21 Club

SMOKED SCOTCH
1 ounce Scotch whisky
Splash of peach schnapps
Splash of Cointreau
1 ounce lemon/lime sour mix

Combine all ingredients with ice in a small glass shaker. Shake vigorously, strain, and pour into a two- to three-ounce carafe. Rest the carafe in a wide-mouthed sherbet glass filled with dry ice, add a small amount of warm water to the dry ice, and watch the smoke appear!
Created by Tim Reid
The Russian Tea Room

SCOTTISH SUMMER
2 ounces Scotch whisky
3/4 ounce Lochan Ora
1 to 1 1/4 ounces fresh lemon juice

Combine all ingredients, and shake well. Serve over ice in a tall glass, and garnish with an orange slice.
Created by James Kelly
The Four Seasons

WHITE FOGG FIZZ
2 ounces Scotch whisky
Juice of a small lime
1 teaspoon sugar
White of one egg
2 tablespoons heavy cream

Combine all ingredients, and shake with both crushed and cubed ice until frosty. Strain into a highball glass with or without ice. Top with a splash of soda, and garnish with a sprig of mint.
Created by Dale De Groff
The Rainbow Room

SMOKED APPLE
2 ounces Scotch whisky
1 ounce Calvados
1 teaspoon sugar
1 1/2 ounces apple juice
Dash of grenadine for colouring

Combine ingredients with ice, and shake well until frosty. Serve over ice in a stem glass.
Created by Robert Castleberry
Carolina

HIGHLANDER ICED COFFEE
1 1/2 ounces Scotch whisky
1/2 ounce dark cocoa
4 ounces iced coffee (or espresso)
Whipping cream

Combine whisky, cocoa, and coffee, and pour into a bell stem or highball glass. Add a dollop of whipped cream. (To enhance the flavour of the cream, add a few drops of vanilla while whipping.)
Created by Michael McCann
Smith & Wollensky

❖

COOKING WITH SCOTCH WHISKY

HIGHLAND PRAWNS
8 ounces prawns
8 ounces new potatoes, diced
1 small onion chopped
2 tablespoons Scotch whisky
1 ounce butter
5 ounces double cream
2 ounces grated cheddar cheese

Fry the onion gently in the butter until soft. Add the potatoes and prawns, and continue cooking until everything is heated through. Add the cream and whisky, season with salt and pepper, and shake the pan gently. Pour into a fireproof dish, cover with grated cheese, and put under a hot grill until cheese is bubbling.

CLEIKUM CLUB LOBSTER
1 fresh lobster
10 ounces cream
3 tablespoons butter
4 tablespoons malt whisky

Cut the lobster lengthwise down the middle, and remove the meat from the tail, claws, and head; cut the meat into chunks. Heat the butter, add the lobster, and season. Warm the whisky, pour it over the lobster, and set light to it. Add cream, heating gently but not letting it boil, to avoid curdling. Serve in the half-shells of the lobster.

SKIRLIE
5 ounces oatmeal
1 medium onion, finely chopped
1 tablespoon chopped fresh herbs
2 ounces butter
2 tablespoons whisky

Combine the onion, oatmeal, butter, and herbs, and season. Mix well with the whisky. Use as poultry stuffing.

TWEED KETTLE
3 pounds salmon
2 shallots, chopped
2 tablespoons chopped parsley
3 tablespoons cream
4 tablespoons whisky

Put the salmon into a fish kettle, cover with cold water, add seasoning, and simmer for five minutes. Remove the salmon after it has cooled, keeping the stock. Remove all skin and bones from the fish, and cut into cubes. Put it into a saucepan with a cup of the fish stock, the shallots, and the whisky. Cover and simmer slowly for twenty minutes. Add the cream, and heat through. Serve either hot or cold.

CHICKEN WITH WHISKY, ALMONDS, AND HONEY

1 chicken for roasting, about 3 pounds
3 tablespoons honey
2 ounces blanched almonds
2 tablespoons oil
3 tablespoons whisky

Rub the bird well with whisky, and season. Line a roasting tin with enough foil to cover the whole bird. Stand the bird on the foil, and add the remainder of the whisky. Rub the honey over the breast and legs, and sprinkle with the almonds. Pour the oil over the bird, wrap it well in the foil, and bake in a moderate oven for about an hour and a half. Open the foil for the last few minutes of cooking to brown the chicken.

BLACK BUN

Pastry:
10 ounces plain flour
1 teaspoon baking powder
4 ounces butter
Salt and pepper
Filling:
8 ounces plain flour
1/2 ounce ground ginger
1/2 ounce ground cinnamon
1/2 teaspoon cream of tartar
1/2 teaspoon baking soda
1 ounce mixed, chopped peel
1 ounce almonds, chopped
1 pound seedless raisins
1 pound currants
1 tablespoon whisky
Milk to mix

To make the pastry, sift the flour, baking powder, and some salt into a bowl, then rub in the butter. Mix with water to make pastry dough. Roll out two-thirds of the dough thinly, and line an eight-inch buttered cake tin along the bottom and up the sides to a height of three inches. For the filling, sift the flour, ginger, cinnamon, cream of tartar, baking soda, and a little pepper. Add peel, almonds, raisins and currants. Mix in whisky and enough milk to give a dropping consistency. Spread the mixture out smoothly into the cake tin. Roll out the rest of the pastry, and fit on top. Trim the edges with a fork. Bake on a low shelf in the oven for four hours at 310°.

CREPES MARY STUART

Batter:
4 ounces plain flour
1 egg
1 egg yolk
1 ounce melted butter
7 ounces creamy milk
Syrup:
1 ounce loaf sugar
1 small orange
Half a lemon
2 ounces butter
5 ounces Scotch whisky

Beat egg and yolk together, and add to sifted flour, along with the butter and half the milk. Beat well until smooth, and then stir in the rest of the milk. Pour enough batter into an oiled and heated pan to cover the base thickly. Fry lightly on one side, then turn over and fry on the other side. Fold in half and keep warm. Continue in this way until all the batter has been used, piling the crêpes on top of one another as they are made. Rub the sugar over the surfaces (washed) of the orange and lemon to remove the zest. Squeeze the juice from the orange and lemon. Place sugar, juice, whisky, and butter in omelette pan. Heat until just boiling. Lift each crêpe into this syrup and coat on each side until heated thoroughly. Fold each one in four, and continue until all have been reheated and fried in the syrup. Serve over-lapping in a silver dish, and, if you wish, pour a glass of whisky over them and ignite.

SKYE DELIGHT

1 teaspoon gelatin
8 ounces milk
2 ounces bitter chocolate
5 ounces cream
2 ounces flaked brown almonds
3 ounces Scotch whisky
1 ounce sugar
6 peach halves
3 ounces peach juice
2 tablespoons Scotch whisky
1 ounce flaked chocolate

Place gelatin in pan and add milk. Stir over a gentle heat until steaming. Break chocolate into small pieces and add to pan. Stir until dissolved, but do not boil. Chill until just set. Whip cream until double its bulk, and fold into the milk with the almonds, three ounces of whisky, and sugar. Pour into an ice-cream or ice-cube tray, and place in the freezer set at its lowest setting. Allow to firm, then turn into a large bowl and beat with a wooden spoon until smooth. Put the mixture back in the tray in the freezer at normal setting. Lay peach halves in a deep glass dish and cover with the juice mixed with the tablespoons of whisky. Spoon the ice cream over them, and dust with flaked chocolate.

TULCHAN LODGE
NUTTY BUMBLE WHISKY CAKE

Meringue:
4 egg whites
8 ounces sugar
4 ounces ground walnuts
Filling:
4 ounces sugar
4 tablespoons water
4 tablespoons hot black coffee
3/4 pint double cream, whipped
1 1/2 to 2 tablespoons malt whisky

Whip egg whites until stiff. Add eight tablespoons of sugar and continue whipping. Fold in remaining sugar with ground almonds. Spread the meringue mixture into two eight-inch rounds on a baking sheet lined with wax paper. Bake at 275° for one and a half to two hours. For the filling, dissolve the sugar in water slowly, then cook to a rich brown caramel. Remove, add coffee, cool. Fold the whipped cream into the caramel mixture. Add the whisky to taste. Sandwich the whisky cream between the two layers of meringue, retaining enough for the sides and the top.

Index